The Playful Adult

10649227

The

Playful
Adult

*500 Ways to Lighten Your Spirit
and Tickle Your Soul*

Sue Baldwin

INSIGHTS Training & Consulting
Stillwater, Minnesota

© 2002 by Sue Baldwin. All rights reserved. No part of this publication may be used or reproduced in any manner whatsoever without written permission, except in the case of brief quotations embodied in critical articles and reviews. For further information, please contact the publisher.

Published by:
INSIGHTS Training & Consulting
2559 Hawthorne Lane, Stillwater, MN 55082-5266
Phone/Fax: 651-439-4100.
E-mail: baldwin@visi.com
Website: www.suebaldwin.com

Cover design and illustrations: Amy Kirkpatrick
Cover illustration: Steve Campbell, Artville
Book design: Dorie McClelland, Spring Book Design

Publisher's Cataloging-in-Publication
(Provided by Quality Books, Inc.)

Baldwin, Sue.
    The playful adult : 500 ways to lighten your spirit
and tickle your soul / Sue Baldwin. -- 1st ed.
    p .cm.
    ISBN 0-9654439-2-2

    1. Wit and humor--Psychological aspects.
    2. Self-actualization (Psychology). 3. Stress management.
    I. Title.
    BF575.L3B35 2002   152.4'3
                                QB133-630

Printed in the United States of America
05   04   03   02   6   5   4   3   2   1

This book is dedicated to my three grandchildren:
Nicholas Timothy Scheel,
Anna Christine Scheel, and
Ellie Sue Scheel.

They are my inspiration for having fun and being playful
on a daily basis. These young people teach me
the importance of living a balanced lifestyle.

CONTENTS

THANK YOU . . .

When I self-publish a book, it takes an entire team to get the book from my thoughts and into your hands. I would like to thank the following people who had fun and contributed as team members to *The Playful Adult*.

Mary Steiner Whelan, Developmental Editor
Andrea McCready, Copy Editor
Amy Kirkpatrick, Graphic Artist
Dorie McClelland, Layout and Design
Margie O'Loughlin, Photographer

The following creative people offered their suggestions for playful activities:

Deb Allemang	Marilyn Johnson
Carrie Baldwin	Pat Landy
Vicki Bliss	Judy Lindman
Patricia Brokman	Joan Mick
Mary Chapman	Diane Olivieri
Jean Dunn	Colleen Pachel
Mary Jean Dunn	Heather Sanders
Sue Dzwnik	Kris Scheel
Michelle Emerling	Joe Sletten
Jody Hermanson	Cheryl Smith
Barb Howe	Mary Steiner Whelan

INTRODUCTION

As I think about the purpose for writing a book about play, I reflect on the early care and education field, in which professional teachers and caregivers work with children daily. The children's work is play. Their teachers' work is to facilitate the play to enhance the children's development and learning. In other words, the adults play, too. When I visit early care programs, I am often struck by the fact that we adults find it easy to play with children. And, yet, we often do not allow ourselves play time.

Perhaps we don't play because, as we grow up, most of us learn to become "responsible." In the process, we forget about the value of play. Play keeps us fit physically, emotionally, intellectually, and spiritually. Without play, we get sick more often, we are less productive, and we sometimes become plain old grumpy.

Being the oldest of four children and the only girl, I felt it was my job to help raise my siblings. Like many other first-born children, I found that play did not come as easily for me as responsibility. As a teenager, I was busy with school, friends, baby-sitting, and helping the family. I was an adult before I learned that a balanced life includes responsibility *and* play.

As a cancer survivor, I know that stress can be detrimental to our health and well-being, and that play helps to reduce stress. This book is designed to encourage people of all ages to play. It will help serious and intense people learn to incorporate silliness, humor, and fun into their daily lives.

I believe we all can learn how to play. I have friends who missed their late-teens silliness because they married young. But now they are in their 40s, their children are gone, and they are making up for lost time.

Some people begin to play with gusto when they are senior citizens. Why wait? Read a few topics in this book today and try some of the *play·time* tips. If you do, I can almost guarantee that tomorrow and every day after that, you will find time to play. It is simply so much fun!

HOW TO USE THIS BOOK

There are fifty everyday life topics in this book. Each topic begins with a quote, followed by a brief narrative about the topic, and at least ten *play·time* tips. That's over five hundred practical, creative ways to bring play into your life! And there is extra space in many *play·time* sections for you to add your own creative ideas.

This is a play reference book. You might want to look at the topics before you go to bed at night or right when you wake up in the morning. If you try out one or two *play·time* tips each day, then you will be a playful adult! Have fun with this book. You will enjoy being more playful, and you will live a healthy and fun life. Now, **let's play!**

You ever heard of Freud airlines?
They have two sections. Guilt
and non-guilt. The seats go all
the way back . . . to childhood.
Ellen Orchid

Airports and Airplanes

I am writing about this topic while I sit in an airport. I am on my way home from a working vacation (is that an oxymoron?). The airport is buzzing with activity. The people who work here and the airline customers all seem to be in their own little worlds of concerns and tasks.

I have a lot of waiting time in airports and on the plane during this trip. What to do to make it fun? Browsing and walking through the airport is a great distraction. It is fun to see both the major retail companies and the local stores. You can imagine what you would buy if you were a billionaire. And, if you don't have time to finish your shopping in the airport, you can do more shopping on the plane. Magazines and catalogues on airplanes give you the opportunity to shop while flying.

You'll find many other options for passing the time. Some people read the newspapers that fellow travelers have left behind, some take a quick nap, and some chat with friends on their cellular phones. Other travelers play cards, tell jokes, or share memories of their trips.

Eating is always an option. Airports offer a variety of foods. Fast food is usually everywhere, but many airports now include more interesting foods, from sushi to lasagna. The smell of cinnamon rolls baking is comforting. Even if you don't indulge in those wonderful, frosting-slathered goodies, you can spend time remembering your mother's kitchen or your favorite bakeries.

People also carry their own snacks to fit their personal diets. Before leaving for a trip, they enjoy collecting food that they will look forward to eating. Some people bring snacks to share with other passengers to build goodwill and start conversations.

It is possible to relax and enjoy the flying experience. Here are some suggestions for having fun in the airport and on the airplane.

play·time

Watch people and create stories about their lives.

Browse through stores that have books and music.

Put on earphones and listen to your favorite tunes.

Develop a wish list from the on-flight shopping magazine.

Bring humorous books or mindless magazines that you might not read at other times.

Listen to the different languages and dialects of people around you and guess where they are from.

Bring a deck of cards or a travel-size board game and play either by yourself or with others.

Take a nap after you decide what you want to dream about.

Develop a ritual that you do each time at the airport (for example, you could buy a cinnamon roll and a magazine to pass the time).

Take a walk on the moving sidewalks.

Imagine the person you would most like to meet in the world is waiting for you. Imagine what the two of you would say.

When traveling with children, bring toys that keep them busy. Happy small travelers make happy adult passengers.

Count how many people are using cellular phones.

Eavesdrop on phone conversations.

While you are waiting for your suitcase at the carousel, watch the other passengers and try to match people with their suitcases.

_____

_____

_____

_____

When you live alone, you can
be sure that the person who
squeezed the toothpaste tube in
the middle wasn't committing
a hostile act.

Ellen Goodman

Alone Time

For some people, being alone can be a real treat; for others, being alone is scary or lonely. Let's look at some of the ways that being alone can enhance playfulness.

Sometimes we feel too inhibited and grown up to act silly, bizarre, or childlike around other adults. We are bombarded with tapes in our heads that say, "What would people think?" I say, let loose and go wild! Do things by yourself that set you free and tickle your spirit. Ask yourself what you want to do to re-create your happy childhood days. When you watch children playing, what do you wish you could still do? I know adults who are great at playing alone. They are responsible adults, but they have a little child in them who is alive and appreciative of all the times they can go out and play.

play·time

Dance naked in the living room.

Lie on a blanket outside and read a book.

Write poetry that is all about you.

Use a soft cushion for protection, and stand on your head.

Make yourself a pizza with lots of toppings and savor every bite.

Turn a somersault on your bed.

Eat a peach without using your hands.

See whether you can blank out your mind for one minute. Can you increase the time?

Sing opera.

Make footprints in snow, mud, or sand, and walk backwards in your own prints.

Sit next to a stream or lake and skip rocks.

_____

_____

_____

_____

A will finds a way.
Orison Swett Marden

Attitude

Some people, unlike you, will never look at this book. They may think they could never be playful or that playing is a waste of time. I believe anyone can be playful—with the right attitude. And, I think play is a good use of time at any age. A playful attitude can lengthen our lives and make them more worth living.

I am like my grandmother Meme. She knew how to have a good time! Meme lived to be ninety-eight years old, and for most of those years, she lived alone. The first woman food broker in America, she supported herself and often my parents and our family. She had a great attitude about play, balance, and maintaining a healthy lifestyle.

I remember her playing cards, golfing, and bowling when she was in her eighties. She continues to be a role model for me. When I start to feel old, sore, or tired, I think about Meme and her positive zest for living.

Attitude is like the rudder on a sailboat. It keeps life on an even keel. We choose our attitude every day. We can choose to be stuffy, to believe that play is for children only. Or we can choose to be vibrant, to believe that play helps us stay young at any age. Having a playful attitude will keep us on a healthy and happy course.

Charles Swindoll wrote a wonderful essay about attitude. He tells us we are in charge of our attitude, and that no one can force us to act or behave in ways we do not choose. Life is ten percent what happens to us and ninety percent our attitude.

When I work with people on team building, attitude comes up every time. Our attitude affects everyone around us. We can choose to be grumpy, sarcastic, stuffy, or moody. We can also choose to be playful, fun loving, relaxed, and youthful. The response and cooperation of others is often a reflection of our attitude.

The choice is yours. How are you going to approach your daily life? What will your attitude be when dealing with personal and professional relationships? You have the power to choose a positive attitude!

So, grab your bubbles, put on a furry boa, and go take on the day.

play·time

If your children complain about what you made them for dinner, ask them to find ONE thing that they like about the meal.

Say out loud, "I can choose to be happy!"

If you have a cold and are feeling ugly, put on a red foam nose.

Wear a button that says "I CAN DO ANYTHING I CHOOSE TO DO!"

Play happy children's music and sing along.

Focus on fun upcoming events in your day: going to dinner with a friend, seeing your pet, or spending some quality time alone.

Spend an hour with a young child. It's hard to feel depressed around a four-year-old.

Make plans to be with someone who is happy and joyful.

Post clever affirmations around your home, vehicle, and office to remind yourself to have fun, play, and enjoy life.

Order tickets to a fun play or musical.

_____

_____

_____

_____

There is no such thing as balance. How I long for that sense of repose after a good day's work. Does anyone have it?

Naomi Thornton

Balance

Creating balance in our lives is the main focus of this book. Becoming playful brings us balance. We can't feel stressed and relaxed at the same time. It is vital to our physical, emotional, and spiritual well-being that we develop ways to compensate for life's intensities. Achieving balance is easier for some people than for others.

I grew up in a family with a very strong work ethic. My father said that work came before play. Make your bed before you go to school. Clean up your room before you go outside to play. As I matured and became my own person, I rethought this philosophy. I learned that play is an important part of our lives, and that we must include it in our daily our schedules.

Many adults who feel very comfortable working, can't easily play. There are exceptions. One of my friends, a nursery school teacher, excels at balancing her lifestyle. Her career focuses around play, and she carries her work philosophy into her personal life. When we incorporate play into our lives, as she does, our family members learn that play can come before work.

Wouldn't it be a great if schools allowed children to play as much as they work? Experienced, playful teachers could teach that playing is an important part of learning. Students would be encouraged to lighten up.

In college, I considered majoring in the newly emerging field of recreation. I thought it would be exciting to teach others playful life skills to use in their personal and professional lives. Then, one day, I realized that if I pursued a recreation career, I would be working while the students were playing. I didn't think I could handle that! So, I moved on to another major.

We cannot store balance up and hope we find time for it on the weekends. That kind of thinking leaves us stressed and out of balance. We need to achieve balance daily. Eventually, it becomes part of our routine.

Here is an exercise that can help you to integrate play into your life. Draw a circle. The circle represents your daily activities. Make a pie chart that indicates how you want to live your life. What percentage of each day do you want to devote to work, family, friends, volunteering, routine, and, of course, play?

At the end of each day, record what you really did. Was your life balanced that day? What can you do to make it more balanced tomorrow? If you do this exercise for two weeks, you will probably become happier and more relaxed, and so will the people around you.

I believe that life is full of choices. We can choose to lead a balanced life!

play·time

To begin to bring balance to your life, play the opposite game:

If you usually plan a lot of activities with friends and family, schedule alone time that is just for you.

Instead of spending ten dollars on something you don't need, give ten dollars to a charity.

For one day, try to play for as many hours as you work.

If you usually feel stressed, do some form of relaxation. You might want to try yoga, tai chi, or massage.

If you feel drained from helping others, ask someone to help you do something, like yard work or making a meal.

If you are feeling trapped, de-clutter your bedroom and enjoy the simplicity that the emptiness creates.

If you usually listen when you have a conversation with a friend, talk instead.

If you usually talk, listen.

If you usually read serious books, read a humorous one.

If you usually watch television, turn it off and tell someone a joke or sing out loud.

If you think the world is against you, go for a walk and look for birds, bugs, and flowers.

If you feel out of balance, stand on one foot and then the other.

_____

_____

_____

_____

Rubber Duckie you're the one.
You make bath time lots of fun.
Ernie from Sesame Street

Bathtub Play

I grew up in a house with six people and one bathroom. We had one bathtub and no showers. Since I was the only girl, I had my bath time alone. I loved to play in that old tub. I made whiskers with soap bubbles and used my washcloth to decorate the wall with soap designs.

Both of my children are girls, so they often shared their bath time when they were young. I would hear giggling, laughter, screeching, and expressions of pure joy as they creatively engaged in bathtub activities.

My grandchildren love to bring as many of their battery-free toys as they can fit into their bathtub. They also have plastic shapes that they stick on the wall to design their bathtub artwork. The art lasts until the next bathtub inhabitant creates new designs.

Our family passes two bathtub activities down from generation to generation. The first activity is giving swimming lessons to waterproof dolls. I was my daughters' swimming instructor, so I was very amused when I heard them mimic me. They counted to three and then submerged their doll under the layers of bubbles. The second activity is wonderfully silly. When most of the water has drained out, the tub bottom gets slippery. Then the bather lies on her stomach and pushes from one end of the tub to the other saying, "Scootie Bootie, Scootie Bootie." This little ritual marks the end of bath time.

These traditions are over a half century old, and I hope they will be passed on to the next generations.

My friend Vicki says that her evening bath is her favorite time of the day. When the days get shorter in the winter, she enjoys this luxurious time earlier in the day. This is her time alone—away from the telephone, children, washing machine, and other demands. She escapes into her own world of bubbles and warm water. It is easy to buy her gifts because she is always looking for new scents, oils, and lotions for the bathtub.

Bathtubs are for more than cleanliness. They are places where we can relax, play, and wash away the cares of the day.

play·time

Churn the water in your half-full bathtub to fill it high with bubbles. See how many bubbles you can make without overflowing the tub.

Turn off all the lights and place candles in safe areas around the tub.

Have your favorite relaxing music playing in the background.

Make your own bath salts. (See the appendix for a recipe.)

Paint the sides of the bathtub with finger paints. (See the appendix for a recipe.)

Put a blow-up pillow behind your head and relax.

Talk to a good friend on a cordless phone.

Add a small amount of food coloring to change the color of the water.

Soak your washcloth in hot water and give yourself a facial.

Submerge yourself under water and hum your favorite silly song.

Use bath balls (made from concentrated soap) that fizz in warm water.

_____

_____

_____

_____

It's lovely, when I forget all birth-
days, including my own, to find
that somebody remembers me.
Ellen Glasgow

Birthdays

Birthdays! What great occasions for play! Birthdays are a time for you to celebrate, from the first day of your life into old age.

When I was a child, each person in the family got to choose the restaurant for their birthday celebration. My favorite restaurant played a recorded birthday song when the candlelit cake arrived at the end of dinner. The song seemed to last forever, and the longer it played, the more embarrassed I became. Now, servers come to the table and sing to the birthday person. The embarrassment is the same and so is the fun.

When each of my grandchildren was born, we celebrated in the hospital. When my youngest grandchild, Ellie, was born, both sets of grandparents, her siblings, and parents celebrated with cupcakes that her older siblings, Nick and Anna, made for her. Although Ellie didn't know what was happening, the video and pictures will amuse her for years. She will also realize that people welcomed her with joy.

We have a local television station that celebrates children's first birthdays. The children's pictures are on the early morning news show. The commentators read some of the highlights of the child's first year. You can see whether your local stations provide this service for the special little ones in your area. If they don't, you can suggest that they do. Let them know that many viewers will tune in to see a favorite one-year-old on TV.

At childcare centers, nursery schools, and elementary schools, the teachers often do special things to honor a child's birthday. They might make special birthday hats, share treats, have a place where the child can display family photos, and allow the child to be the leader for the day.

I frequently see the exteriors of homes decorated for birth-days. The decorations sometimes encourage people to honk their horns in honor of the day or to enjoy the balloons, banners, or yard signs that say it is a day to celebrate someone's life.

You can celebrate your birthday by yourself or with friends and family. My friend Joe decided on his twenty-ninth birthday to do something special to mark the end of his twenties. He went skydiving. He will never forget the day, and his friends and family celebrated with him while watching the video-taped record of his achievement.

Celebrate being forty or fifty or ninety-two! When you have your one hundredth birthday, you can send your name in to be mentioned on national television!

No matter which birthday you are celebrating, it is a special event. You can invent your own celebration or carry on your family traditions. Whatever you do, make your day memorable and playful.

play·time

Allow your friends and family to have a birthday party for you—no matter what your age.

Plan a birthday party for yourself.

On your birthday, take the day off from work and declare it a holiday.

Call your mom and thank her for your birth.

Test-drive your favorite dream car.

Get a massage or a manicure.

Bring a special cake to work to celebrate.

Honor the birthday person with breakfast in bed.

Find three restaurants: one that offers free breakfasts, another that offers free lunches, and another that offers free dinners to birthday celebrants. Eat all three meals at different restaurants for free.

Plan special trips to honor milestone birthdays.

_____

_____

_____

_____

Just the knowledge that a good book is awaiting one at the end of a long day makes that day happier.

Kathleen Norris

Books

When I was a very young child, I wasn't interested in books. Running around outside and playing were much more fun. My attitude changed in third grade when I read my first chapter book. *Heidi* introduced me to the imagination, relaxation, and pure pleasure of reading. I am still hooked. I am always reading one book while I have another one waiting by my bed.

For a while, I read every self-help and diet book in print. Soon they all began to sound the same. I realized it didn't matter how many self-help books I read, I was going to help myself!

Now, I read fiction to totally escape life's stressors. The type of fiction doesn't matter, as long as the characters are fascinating. During the months I went through chemotherapy, some people I volunteer with got me started on a mystery series by a woman writer. As soon as I finished one paperback, two more were waiting for me. The books were a great distraction. By the end of my treatments, I had read the whole collection.

It is interesting to listen to friends, or even strangers, talk about their favorite books and authors. My friend Ruth, who is visually impaired, is an avid reader. She devours books by listening to them on tape. Her intensity reminds me of the way I listened to the radio when I was young. My imagination created vivid images as I listened. Ruth has readers, including her husband, who help her stay up-to-date on current events. Through them, she reads several newspapers from the Internet.

Recently, a group of my friends began a book club. We hold our monthly meetings in members' homes. Each month's host chooses the book the group will read. We can choose any kind of book, as long as it is a paperback available at a bookstore and at the library.

There are many ways get together with books. If you use the library, reading can be free. Whatever, however, you read, you will have fun and add new interests to your life.

play·time

Carry a book with you at all times. You never can tell when you will have extra time to read.

Spend time at your local library roaming through the shelves of books. Close your eyes and pick out a book to read.

Start a book club with a group of friends. Enjoy reading and discussing books you might not choose to read on your own.

Curl up with a book and a bowl of flavored popcorn, and enjoy.

Go to your favorite bookstore and browse. Buy a cup of coffee or cider at the bookstore café, and then sit down and sample different kinds of books.

Pack a bag of your favorite children's books and read to children at a childcare center.

When you are driving, listen to audio cassettes or CDs of your favorite books.

Cuddle with a child (any age) and read wonderful books.

Read a chapter book with a child. Take turns reading.

Always pass a good book, not just the title, on to another person.

E-mail meaningful quotes from books to your friends, or send them the quotes in cards or letters.

Make your own books using photos of favorite friends, family members, and pets.

Create a memory book of only positive and happy thoughts and experiences.

Talk to family members and gather stories to create a family memory book similar to a family recipe book.

Go through old books and look for pressed flowers and family keepsakes.

Add flowers and keepsakes to your favorite books so that others can enjoy discoveries.

Read your favorite childhood books to an unborn baby.

_____

_____

_____

_____

Youth is not a time of life;
it is a state of mind.
Samuel Ullman

Bubbles

Over the years, I have given hundreds of presentations nationally and internationally. During that time, I have developed a trademark. Bubbles! I talk about them, play with them, and take them wherever I go. I also bring them out during times of personal and professional stress and turmoil.

Bubbles started out being a child's toy. I, however, did not learn to appreciate them until I was an adult. I like bubbles because they are fun, harmless, tasteful, easy to make, and inexpensive to buy. Bubbles make everyone smile. I think that makes the world a healthier and happier place.

Environmentalists say that rice and balloons are not good to have at weddings, because they harm the environment. Blowing bubbles at the bride and groom after the ceremony is a safe way for people to express their joy. There are small, individualized bubble containers designed for weddings. Some are shaped like churches, others like bells or flowers. Rarely is all of the solution used at the wedding. The next time you attend a wedding, offer to collect the partially used bubble containers. These small containers make it easier to travel with bubbles. Keep them in your pocket, purse, briefcase, or fanny pack. Then you can bring them out whenever you feel the need.

One of my favorite places to carry bubbles is in the glove compartment of my car. I do not blow bubbles while I am driving, but I often give them to restless children or bored passengers. When I am stuck in a traffic jam, I roll down the window (this is a very important first step) and blow bubbles for others to enjoy. It usually brings a strange look, followed by a smile, from the other drivers.

Another favorite place I use my bubbles is on shopping excursions with my mother or youngest daughter. They both love to spend a lot of time in dressing rooms and then want my opinion the clothes. I am not a petite person, so I get bored looking at tiny clothes. So, while I am sitting on the floor in the dressing room, out come the bubbles! It is so convenient to have a little travel-size bubble container with you at all times. You never know when you might want to blow some bubbles.

I am passing on my love of bubbles to my grandchildren, so that they can develop a bubble passion early. I hope bubbles will be a part of my legacy that continues for generations.

play·time

Make bubbles out of soap detergent. (See the appendix for a recipe.)

Use hangers and a large container of bubble solution to make huge bubbles.

Describe what the bubble formations look like. Do they look like people? Animals?

Blow bubbles while you are in line at the grocery store, at the bus stop, in the doctor's or dentist's office, in your car in the parking lot, outside in a cool breeze, or in a rowboat in the middle of a glassy lake.

Have a bubble-blowing contest with children or friends. See who can blow the biggest, smallest, or highest bubble.

Take bubbles to a nursing home and let the wonderful seniors rediscover their childhoods.

Bring bubbles out to soothe a troubled child.

Use bubbles as a transition activity with children when moving from one event to another.

Name the colors that are in your bubbles.

Blow bubbles from in front of a fan.

You can't stay young forever,
but you can be immature for
the rest of your life.

Maxine Wilkie

Childhood Games

I vividly remember the speaker at my daughter's seventh-grade graduation. He said to the adolescents who were beginning their twelve-week summer vacation, "Only boring people get bored." A very short and powerful statement I have remembered often throughout the years.

When I remember my childhood days, I recall games that required nothing but an active imagination. Many of these games were passed down from generation to generation. My fear is that we will forget these simple pleasures.

When I was growing up, children played, free of cares. Our only restriction was to tell our parents where we were going. We had to be in the house right after the streetlights went on. The first child to notice the streetlights go on yelled, "Lights on!" and was the day's winner.

In the summer, the neighborhood children played outside, unsupervised, from early morning until bedtime. Games like basketball, volleyball, soccer, croquet, tetherball, badminton, kick-the-can, tennis, and catch took place at the spur of the moment. There was no need for adults to organize the activities. Children used their imaginations to have fun with very little or no money. "Oh, the times they are a changin'," as Bob Dylan sings.

We can reintroduce the simple joys of playing. We can pass on yo-yo games, hopscotch, tag, wagons, scooters, bicycles, rope swings, kick-the-can, jacks, marbles, tiddlywinks, jump ropes, paper dolls, checkers, and tic-tac-toe. Before it's too late, we can let children and adults know that fun doesn't have to be organized, electronic, or expensive. Here are some ways you can play childhood games by yourself or with your friends and family, whatever their ages.

play·time

Talk with someone older than you and ask them about how they played when they were a child.

Make paper dolls.

Use a rock and draw a hopscotch pattern on the sidewalk.

Draw a circle on concrete or in dirt and shoot marbles.

Play rope games by yourself or with a friend. (Libraries have books that teach these games.)

Find an old tree and climb as high as you dare to go.

Build a fort outside from scrap lumber.

Build a fort inside with card tables and sheets or blankets.

Camp out in a sleeping bag under the stars.

Play "Mother may I?" with silly requests.

Go outside with a bat and ball and ask others to join you in a game.

Use a wagon to collect your leaves.

Kick a can around the street and tell those peeking out of their windows to come on out and play.

Set up a card table in the front yard and invite friends to a game of checkers.

_____

_____

_____

_____

Your clothes speak
even before you do.
Jacqueline Murray

Clothes

A decade or two ago, we had black clothes in our closet to wear to funerals. Now we wear black because it is slimming and attractive. Many women wear black professionally and casually. Most have one little (or not so little) black dress for special occasions.

My friend Diane's entire wardrobe is black. Being a playful adult, Diane adds fun accents to her slimming black clothes. She wears bright scarves, funky pins, and shoes that add pizzazz.

Sometimes a person's workplace dictates the standard for professional dress. And, sometimes, there are ways to vary the standards. I feel comfortable when my physician wears a sports shirt and casual slacks. I know he has the required white coat somewhere in his office. But when he is treating patients, his casual clothes send a professional yet nonthreatening message.

Childcare professionals love special days, such as pajama, funny hat, beach, and backwards days. On those days, they can come to work dressed in fun clothes, just like the kids. What a job benefit!

My personal and professional wardrobes exude fun and playfulness. I wear bright primary colors that tell the world I really do have a passion for fun. I accessorize with fanciful pins and colorful earrings. Part of the fun is collecting jewelry and other extra touches at art fairs, boutiques, and garage sales.

One of the many joys of aging is that we no longer care so much about peer pressure. We can dress the way we want, whatever our profession. I hope the following tips help you to dress and live more playfully.

play·time

Go to a sale rack in a shoe department. Buy eye-catching, yet comfortable shoes that you wouldn't buy if you had to pay full price.

Decorate a pair of white tennis shoes with glitter and paint.

Have a shirt-decorating party with friends. Use fabric paint and your imagination to create wearable art.

Wear tee shirts printed with fun messages.

Wear ties or scarves with bright colors, cartoon characters, or sports images.

Express yourself by wearing wild baseball caps. They come decorated with everything from sequins to fake fur animal tails.

Wear cute button covers on your plain shirts.

Get a plain denim shirt embroidered with a design that is "you."

Wear funny animal-shaped slippers out to dinner or a movie.

On occasions when you must be prim and proper, put on your Wonder Woman or Superman underwear. Only you will know, and you will enjoy the formal event much more.

_____

_____

_____

_____

Every child is an artist. The problem is how to remain an artist once he grows up.

Pablo Picasso

Creative Art

Even if you are not an accomplished artist, you can have artistic fun. Spontaneous and simple activities such as building sand-castles, finger-painting, or drawing with magic markers are all creative art.

If you ask a room full of adults how many of them are artists, only a few people raise their hands. If you ask children how many of them are artists, they all raise their hands. Free from adult expectations, they know that they create beautiful things.

Three-year-old Anna loves to use scissors to add finishing touches to her colorful artwork. She cuts tiny fringes all around the paper and tickles her fingers with them.

Six-year-old Nick loves to make scary designs on paper. Then he folds the paper and flies his creations across the living room. Any paper is an opportunity for him to create magical flying things.

We adults need to remember what it was like when we were little and uninhibited. Then our creativity flows. Cooking creatively, arranging a collage, sewing a Halloween costume, stenciling a bedroom wall, or hand-painting a china plate all express our creativity. We can let go of our fears of making a mistake and just have fun.

I am writing this book during a working vacation in the Caribbean. Yesterday, I was walking along the beach. It was deserted except for smooth white sand and piles of discarded rocks and shells. Walking the same beach this morning, I noticed that someone had put one of the largest rocks on end so that it is pointing up to the blue sky. This afternoon, fifteen more rocks have been added, creating an amazing rock sculpture next to the ocean. It reminds me of the game Jenga, in which you place small blocks on top of each other. This magnificent yet simple sculpture is truly an example of playful adults creating art. It didn't cost one penny, but it is a beautiful creation that hundreds of people will enjoy.

We are all artists. I hope that the following suggestions will open up your childlike creativity.

play·time

Make or buy frosting to decorate a cake or homemade cookies.

Buy a bunch of flowers and spend time arranging them.

Weave a basket.

Enroll in watercolor or beginning oil-painting classes at a community education center.

Take photos of people and things that make you smile.

Create a garden inside your home or throw wildflower seeds outside and see what happens.

Get a new set of markers or crayons and draw something you see in your home.

Color outside the lines in a coloring book.

Doodle on a blank piece of paper using many colors.

Make a sandcastle incorporating items from your kitchen.

Draw designs in the dirt with a stick.

Paint your fingernails with a funky color.

Build a sculpture with natural objects such as rocks, twigs, sand, and dirt.

Never lend your car to anyone
to whom you have given birth.
Erma Bombeck

Driving

My "Leave It to Beaver" family owned one station wagon. My father commuted to work by public transportation, so my mother, brothers, and I used the station wagon for family errands and adventures. Like many others of my generation, I learned to drive before I was legally old enough to do so. My mother taught me on the small back roads in Michigan when I was thirteen. I loved to drive. I felt so independent! When I actually got my driver's license, I was off and running. Many decades later, I continue to enjoy driving, although my passion for it is lessening a little as I age.

When my brother Doug and I were young, our family went weekly on the compulsory "Sunday drive." The family piled into the car—parents in the front seat and children in the back. There were no seatbelts then, so my brother and I could move around. When we started fighting with each other, my mother drew an imaginary line down the middle of the back seat that neither of us was supposed to cross. Of course we did, which prompted my parents to use the famous parental phrase, "Don't make me stop this car!"

Despite the squabbles, these drives were enjoyable family bonding times. We drove out into the country (now the site of a mega shopping mall in the Kansas City suburbs). My mother initiated activities to distract us from our bickering. We identified different makes of cars, looked for out-of-state license plates, played twenty questions, sang songs, listened to radio shows, played alphabet and number games using road signs, and heard stories about family history and traditions.

The driving experience has changed with the times. Many families have more than one car. People are more likely to drive alone while they listen to the radio, CDs, or books on tape, or talk on their cellular phones. If a group drives together, passengers can use earphones. Families on long drives can watch videos on a portable TV. Young children can play computer games. Individuals can now choose their own form of driving entertainment. But we may want to occasionally go back to the olden days with family activities that keep family interaction alive, spats and all!

play·time

Take turns humming a favorite song and play "Name That Tune."

Look for letters in the words on road signs, and see who can complete the alphabet first.

Add up the numbers on license plates and see who gets to fifty first.

Look for Volkswagen Beetles. Yell, "Slug bug!" when you see one.

Play "I spy" using objects in the car.

Guess how many miles are left until you reach your destination.

Take a nap with a favorite blanket.

Read a book aloud for everyone to appreciate.

Listen to the "oldies" on the radio.

Guess how many miles you have traveled every half hour.

Count how many kinds of birds, animals, flowers, and trees you see.

_____

_____

I think anyone who comes upon a Nautilus machine suddenly will agree with me that its prototype was clearly invented at some time in history when torture was considered a reasonable alternative to diplomacy.

Anna Quindlen

Exercise

Some people might look scornfully at this topic, wondering how exercise can possibly be fun and playful. Many of us older people think exercising means doing jumping jacks and pushups, as we learned in high school physical education classes. Those classes have changed immensely. Classes now teach sports and activities that children can use for a lifetime.

You can do exercises such as walking, swimming, running, dancing, and weightlifting without joining an organized sport. While I write about this topic, I am watching many people walking alone, or with a friend, on the beach. Other people are taking an early morning swim in the ocean. Their exercise is just as valuable as the leaping and running the volleyball teams will be doing on the beach later in the day.

If weight reduction is important to you, you can look at charts that relate calorie use to exercise. These charts usually include many kinds of exercise. But remember, it is not all about weight. It is also about how good you feel after you begin to exercise. Exercises that encourage relaxation are becoming increasingly popular. These exercises include yoga, tai chi, Pilates, water aerobics, and chi gong. You can check out a video and do these at home, or you can take a class at your local community education center.

My daughter Kris and I belong to the same fitness club. We do mother-daughter bonding at 5:30 a.m. by working out together before we begin our busy daily schedules. Exercising with someone else is a great incentive. Even though I often want to push the snooze button one more time, I know Kris is waiting for me. We talk and laugh while we use the equipment, and we often make funny faces in front of the mirrors when we do our free weights.

"Ball work" is a new, popular way to exercise. Have you ever seen young children bouncing around on an oversized ball called a Hoppity Hop? Now adults can enjoy the same fun and call it exercise. Oversized, rubber balls are available through sporting stores or physical therapy clinics. Adults hop on the giant balls and bounce their way to fun and fitness. Ball work can involve balance, stretching, meditating, weight training, aerobic exercise, or just plain fun at home, the gym, or the physical therapy clinic.

Exercise reduces stress. When I do stress management training, people say they know that they need to exercise, but just can't find the time. If you can make exercise fun, you will be able to find the time.

So what are you waiting for? Find some fun ways to exercise, put this book down for a while, and get started!

play·time

Don't get stuck in a rut. Vary the kinds of exercise you do.

Exercise early in the morning, before your brain is awake and knows what you are doing.

Use some household items, like cans of soup, for weights when you exercise at home.

Check out an assortment of exercise videos from the library.

Dance to funky music, either by yourself or with a child.

Go for a bicycle ride by yourself and listen to nature's sounds.

Bring your bike inside and put it on a stand so you can continue biking during inclement weather.

Wear fun and comfortable outfits while you exercise.

Listen to your favorite music on headphones and sing out loud while you are exercising.

Form an exercise group with friends so you can laugh together as you work out.

Tell funny stories to your exercise buddy when you exercise together. It makes the time go faster!

_____

_____

_____

_____

*Reunions are always fraught
with awkward tensions—the
necessity to account for oneself;
the attempt to find, through
memories, an ember of the old
emotions.*

Anita Shreve

Family Reunions

You may be thinking about having a family reunion, or maybe
you just had a reunion that was a disaster. Whatever your situation, I hope that you will find that these events can be fun.

I want to tell you about the only large family reunion I have
attended. My birthday is in the summer, so we scheduled my
fiftieth birthday party during summer vacation. Finally, all my
friends and family could meet each other.

As my youngest brother, Brian, and his family got out of
their van after a long road trip, his son got the stomach flu. He
was the first of many family members who suffered with flu during the next several days. We checked in with each other daily to
compare symptoms. Only three people escaped the illness. I got
the flu . . . you guessed it . . . on my birthday! A friend just

reminded me that you don't remember events that go perfectly, but you do remember the disasters. That would be true when it came to our family reunion.

Out of every disaster, something good happens. Because so many of us were sick, we couldn't do all of the large-group activities we had planned. Instead, we spent time talking in small groups. We truly enjoyed each other's company and got reacquainted on a personal level. The reunion was a success because we did the most important thing—we celebrated being family!

Families come in all sizes, and so can reunions. Our family reunions are typically small, with me and my three siblings, our small families, and our mother. On the other hand, some families have twelve siblings and dozens of cousins. No matter what the group size, reunions are a great time to pass on family history and to catch up with each other's lives.

A reunion may be the only time some family members get to meet and visit with each other. Some reunions are more formal than others. Some are extravagant combinations of trips and great food. But reunions don't have to be expensive. Tents can be pitched, sleeping bags can be unrolled on the living room floor, and the food can be potluck. Reunions involve communication, organization, and compromise. But the time and effort is worth it. Your family, with all of its idiosyncrasies, is worth it. You will rebuild relationships and have memories that last a lifetime.

play·time

Have a general planning committee, with one member from each family as a representative. Have the committee plan contests, activities, and prizes.

Start a family tree on a large piece of paper and have others add people who are not listed.

Have a golf tournament. Nonparticipants can ride along in golf carts.

Create a slide show from old photographs.

Get different family recipes and prepare special foods that are a part of the family history.

Have everyone bring pictures and compare family resemblances.

Design special tee shirts that list each family member's name.

For large groups, have each family design their own nametags.

Give fun prizes to the youngest, oldest, tallest, or shortest family members.

Plan games for different age groups. Try croquet, Frisbee, or water balloon fights.

Have gunnysack or relay races, mixing up members from different families.

Have a skit night with impromptu suggestions for topics.

Ask the family elders to share their humorous and happy family stories.

_____

_____

_____

_____

Personal ads are dangerous.
You have to separate the ones
who are lying from the ones
who are hallucinating.
Rita Rudner

Flirting

Two-year-olds love to flirt. Why is it, then, that many fifty-year-olds would rather have a root canal than flirt? What happens between two and fifty? Life happens, I guess. Our life experiences often make us too shy to enjoy being flirtatious. I am one of those people. So, I think about flirting the same way as I think about exercising. We can decide that we want to flirt and that it may be fun, and then we go out and do it.

Perhaps I can blame my parents for my flirting phobia. That's it, it's my parents' fault! Just kidding. You see, they did send me to all-girls schools until I went to college. When girls my age were learning how to interact with men, I was busy cross-stitching with the nuns. By the time I attended a coeducational college, my skills in relating to the opposite sex were very limited.

On the other hand, my twenty-eight-year-old daughter, Carrie, who always attended coeducational schools, believes that flirting is a natural part of life. She has been flirting since she was two years old.

Carrie believes it is important to flirt. Flirting, she says, produces endorphins, and makes others feel good, too. The best places to flirt, according to Carrie, my flirting coach, are the unexpected ones. Carrie's thirty-two-year-old, married sister suggested she spend time in places where single men are. Carrie's first thought was to go to a bar. Kris quickly replied, "Do you want to be with a drinker?" and then she suggested that Carrie try the grocery store or the local gym.

Carrie discovered that the grocery store is perfect. She's still learning to cook, so she can always ask for cooking tips. She recommends hanging out in the produce or deli departments, where you are more likely to meet health-conscious and interesting men. Stay away from the chip aisle, where you are likely to find your average couch potato.

I have decided to take both of my daughters' advice and try out this new technique. The next time I go for a bike ride on the nearby bike trail, I am going to say "hi" to everyone I pass. I will also try to maintain eye contact without running my fellow bikers off the narrow path. I will prove that we are never too old to learn new tricks from our children.

Are you inspired to take the plunge? Here are some tips for having fun with flirting.

play·time

Send your personal "résumé" to a prospective beau.

Send a love letter made from those little conversational Valentine hearts. Glue them on construction paper.

Put a love note in a newspaper that your special friend will be sure to read.

Show your genuine interest in an acquaintance's stories. Ask open-ended questions to keep the other person talking.

Smile and give compliments.

Shake hands or gently touch an acquaintance's shoulder.

Do a double-take across a crowded room.

Ask for help from a stranger.

Invite someone out to a park on a Saturday afternoon.

When you are waiting in line, start up a conversation.

Send a thoughtful card to a recent acquaintance.

Send a beverage to a stranger at a restaurant.

Give someone money and ask them to play some music in the jukebox.

True friends are those who really know you but love you anyway.

Edna Buchanan

Friends

When I list the priorities in my life, friends are close to the top. My friends are the family I choose. Friends have been important to me as long as I can remember. I cannot imagine my life without them. I learn so much about human nature from these people—my circle of friends.

Laughter and playing are important components of friendships. Not long ago, I had lunch with two friends. We ate and talked, and we laughed often, and sometimes loudly. A woman at the next table leaned over and told us how much she enjoyed hearing us laugh, because it reminded her of the good times she had with her sister.

Friends can help you laugh the one hundred belly laughs that it takes to raise your endorphins. You know you are having a really good laugh when your smile lines hurt, your stomach muscles and diaphragm ache, and your stress disappears.

Friends keep us balanced and on course. If you have good friends in your life now, cherish them. If you have let friendships go or haven't taken the time to make enough friends, go out now and begin developing some lasting relationships. Then, use the following tips to keep the friendships playful.

play·time

Do something you enjoy, with another person. Go to a play, a garden tour, the theater, or a movie.

Rent a tandem bike and go for a bike ride.

Call a friend on the phone and laugh about silly things.

Spend the day at a spa with a friend.

Play the game "remember when" to relive funny memories.

Go bowling, fishing, or golfing together.

Go out for a group meal that ends with chocolate.

Take a trip or a vacation together.

Form a support group with people who share an experience or interest: parenting, work, exercise, investing, quilting, and traveling.

Make a scrapbook together to remind you of the treasured times you share.

Do something spontaneous together that is fun for both of you: get an ice cream cone, feed the ducks, try on hats, fly kites.

Go for a ride together at an amusement park.

Make up silly nicknames for each other.

Plan a monthly game night with friends.

_____

   _____

_____

   _____

Gardens are the result of a collaboration between art and nature.

Penelope Hobhouse

Gardening

As I am writing about gardening, I am listening to "The Home and Garden Show" on the radio. Gardening is so popular that there are many TV shows, radio programs, and magazines dedicated to it. People of all ages, and all budgets, can garden. Although a green thumb is a plus, desire and interest are really what make gardening successful.

We usually think of gardening outside when the weather is warm. Actually, we can garden year-round and in any climate. For example, preschool children plant seeds indoors in small cups. They watch the seeds sprout and grow, and then they move the fledgling plants into larger pots. Before their very eyes, the plants bloom and grow for a long time.

During my first job working in a childcare center, I was in awe of the many healthy plants in the classrooms. The staff told me that plants thrive in healthy places filled with happy voices. Now, when I visit a home where there are beautiful plants, I envision the people living there singing and speaking happy words to their plants.

I live in a cold climate, so I fill my home with wonderful plants, which keep me company during the long winter months. As soon as the meteorologists assure me that the frost is gone for the year, I send many of my indoor plants outside to camp. And Mother Nature takes care of them for a few months.

One of my favorite gardening activities is planting wildflowers. I throw seeds out in the fall and again in the spring. It's always a surprise to see what flowers pop up later. I don't have to weed the garden in the summer, because the wildflowers take over the open, weedy spaces. The wildness is great fun and gets many compliments from visitors.

When my Uncle Michael lived in California, he had a huge, healthy jade plant outside on his deck facing the ocean. When Michael died, we gave parts of the jade plant to his closest friends and family as a remembrance. My small stem has grown into a healthy, thriving plant that loves to be at camp during the summer. This plant lived outside next to a large pot of impatiens, and somehow some seedlings of the beautiful pink-flowered plant got into the succulent green plant's soil. Now they both live together in the same pot.

Gardening can involve the whole family. It is a hobby that brings happiness not only to the people who do the planting, but also to those who come to see what is growing. Consider doing some of these playful gardening activities.

play·time

Preserve your favorite flowers by pressing them in a book.

Wear a big, frumpy hat while you are working in your garden.

Create fun scarecrow people of different sizes with fun outfits.

Use your computer to learn more about different plants, including everything you need to know about growing indoor and outdoor gardens.

Plant flowers that attract butterflies.

Grow some veggies. Eat some in the summer, and then process and freeze some for soup and stew to eat in the cold of winter.

Give a big bouquet of flowers to a friend.

Watch the bunnies and other wildlife attracted to what you are growing.

Put up a birdhouse and see whether anyone takes up residence.

Paint rocks in bright colors and fun patterns, and place them in your garden.

Plant a theme garden: a butterfly garden, a patriotic garden (rows of red, white, and blue), a pink flamingo garden, a garden of only edible flowers.

Make trellises out of unusual things, like pieces of old metal, odd-shaped branches, colorfully painted wood, bamboo, etc.

Make colorful stepping stones by pressing pieces of colored glass into cement.

Make fun bird feeders and birdhouses out of found objects. Pinecones coated with peanut butter are just one example.

Plant an herb garden.

Plant a trellis in the form of a teepee and put a table and chair in it.

Place colorful annuals in fun pots on your deck.

Paint your lawn chairs with outrageous colors and patterns.

Wear fun clothing while working in your garden.

_____

_____

_____

_____

The closest friends I have made all through life have been people who also grew up close to a loved and loving grandmother or grandfather.

Margaret Mead

Grandparenting

Everything about being a grandmother rocks! I love being called Nana (every family gets to have their special name for grandparents). I love the active role I play in my grandchildren's lives, the childcare, and best of all . . . not being the person who is one hundred percent responsible for my grandchildren's development.

I raised and launched two children, and I firmly believe that parenting is the hardest job anyone will ever have. I also believe grandparenting is the greatest reward for that work.

I was in the room to see each of my grandchildren's three little faces come out of the womb. I have had a deep commitment and attachment to each of them ever since those very special days. My role as Nana is to offer the children guidance and teach them how to have a loving, caring, and playful relationship with an older person. My daughter teaches me that it is the time I spend with the children, not the material things I buy for them, that creates lasting memories. I also know that going shopping occasionally with a grandchild to choose a special toy is fun for everybody.

I make sure each grandchild frequently has one-on-one Nana time. One of my favorite memories is of my mother and my daughter Kris. One day while my mother was visiting, I looked out the window at our tiny patio. Mom was teaching Kris how to skip. Special simple memories can last a lifetime.

When I am with Nick, Anna, and Ellie, I get to act silly and do fun things that create smiles and memories for all of us. I can block out the rest of the world with all of its responsibilities, and just play! Now you can see why I say that being a grandmother rocks!

play·time

Spend quality time with one grandchild at a time.

Play age-appropriate board games.

Play funky music and dance.

Dress up in old clothes you have stored away.

Make up and sing silly songs.

Go for a walk. Skip when walking gets boring.

Go for a bike ride or be brave and try a go-cart.

Sit and rock together, humming lullabies.

Finger-paint with pudding.

Act like a pony and give your grandchildren pony rides.

Look together at photo albums that feature your grandchildren as the stars.

Bake cut-out cookies for no special holiday or reason.

Make gingerbread cookies that look like you and your grandchildren.

Find Black Beauty on the merry-go-round and go for a ride with a grandchild.

Go sliding down water slides or snowy hills.

Search for four-leaf clovers.

Make a train out of the living room chairs.

Hide a piece of gum or candy in your hand and let a grandchild guess which hand holds the treat.

Tell stories to your grandchildren about "the old days."

Make lemonade using real lemons.

Pass on your cultural heritage through songs, games, and food.
Do this often, not just on holidays.

_____

_____

_____

_____

Youth is when you're allowed to stay up late on New Year's Eve. Middle age is when you're forced to.

Bill Vaughn

Holidays

Holidays are a time for celebration. We are all familiar with holidays in our own cultures, and we can always learn about holiday traditions in other cultures. Holiday traditions give us the opportunity for reflection, eating, playing, praying, and being with friends and family.

When I was a child, holidays were a special time to get together. Every year, one of my grandmothers had all of her grandchildren over for an Easter celebration on Good Friday. We gathered at her apartment for a meal, and then we played games with our cousins. We laughed, joked, and felt free to be ourselves without our parents' expectations in the room.

Many people get together to celebrate their cultural backgrounds at holiday times with special food, games, costumes, religious observances, music, and decorations. My friend Jane developed a way to pass on her family's holiday traditions. When each of her children married, she gave them a box of things for various holidays. Some items were new, and some were family treasures. Her special box gave the newlywed couple a way to continue holiday traditions.

Although we look forward to holidays, we also know they can be stressful. I teach a class called "Handling Holiday Stress." One participant told me that a co-worker wanted to attend, but she was too stressed about the upcoming holiday!

Playing is one way to balance holiday stress. If we look at holidays through children's eyes, we may see holidays in a more positive light. Pretend you are a child. What aspects of the holidays are most playful and enjoyable? How can you focus on fun and cut back on stress?

Children tell me that sometimes they dread the holidays because the joy that they anticipated is overshadowed with stress. How important is it that the decorations are perfect, that the gifts are magnificent, or that the table looks like Martha Stewart's? Holiday fun is not about impressing others or doing everything. Holidays are about doing what brings joy and happy memories to you, your family, and friends.

I hope that some of these tips will help you add some playfulness to your holidays.

play·time

Simplify your life by decreasing your list of "have to's."

Build in a nap time for all family members before the special event takes place.

Encourage potluck events so you are not the only one preparing the food.

Save decorations in a special container and bring them out each year.

Rotate the location of the celebration among friends and family members.

Consult with children about how they want to celebrate the holiday.

Put simple seasonal decorations in every room. Don't forget the bathrooms!

Dress up like a holiday character and pay a visit to the children's ward in the hospital.

Invite neighborhood families over for hot chocolate, cookies, and board games.

Have a bake-off. Everyone can swap recipes and make cookies. Fill containers with the cookie varieties and bring them to a shelter or a nursing home.

Go caroling at times other than the traditional holidays.

Dress up for Halloween and surprise the children when you answer your door.

_____

_____

_____

_____

In hospitals there was no time
off for good behavior.
                    Josephine Tey

Hospitals

There are three reasons most of us go to the hospital: to be a
patient, to visit someone, or to volunteer. I have done all three.
I definitely prefer the last two options.

There are many ways you can tickle the souls of patients when
you visit or volunteer. Although many hospitals no longer allow
you to bring in latex balloons, you can bring in Mylar balloons.
These balloons come in wonderful colors and shapes, and they are
often printed with messages that brighten patients' spirits.

When my third grandchild, Ellie, was born, I took her siblings, Anna and Nick, down to the hospital gift store to pick out
their favorite Mylar balloon. After much deliberation, they
decided on a huge red fire engine. It didn't seem to me to have
anything to do with a little girl being born, but it certainly
brightened up the room. And the expressions on Anna and
Nick's faces when they presented the balloon to their mom and
Ellie were priceless.

You can bring other gifts to patients to help lighten their discomfort, or maybe to help them laugh so much that they forget the pain. Displaying get-well cards on the walls and ledges in the room, rather than stacking them in a pile, surrounds a patient with loving, cheerful thoughts. I have a bag of favorite videos I deliver to patients who will be in the hospital for an extended stay. I also bring light magazines on fashion, home decorating, travel, or gossip to relax a patient who might not be able to do serious reading.

Hospital playfulness requires creativity and sensitivity. You need to be in tune with a patient's needs. When my friend Cokie was confined to over three weeks of bed rest before little Wyatt was born, her family and friends thought of creative activities to help her pass the time. Her younger sister decorated the hospital room for Halloween; her older sister brought wonderful children's books for Cokie to read to Wyatt in the womb; her mother read books to Cokie; the baby's father brought their dog for a visit; friends brought all kinds of stuffed animals; and I appeared several times for guided imagery sessions. I also read to her from my book *Lighten Up and Live Longer.*

I hope that you can use some of the following playful ideas the next time you visit or volunteer at a hospital.

play·time

Find the cookies in the surgical waiting room and take one.

Visit the nursery and look at the newborn babies.

Sit in a wheelchair and ride down a ramp.

Watch comedy shows on the television in the waiting room.

Make a homemade bouquet from your garden flowers and take them to the patient. Wildflowers from the side of the road also look great.

Go to the hospital cafeteria and order something that you wouldn't cook at home.

Visit the gift shop. They often have different and unusual items.

Bring your favorite toys to play with.

Bring flowers and ask a nurse to give them to a patient who doesn't have any.

Put removable plastic decals on the windows.

Decorate the room to make it look more like home. Use framed photos, doilies, throw pillows, and knickknacks.

Hire a clown to entertain in the children's ward.

Wear a funny pair of glasses or a red nose and read your favorite
magazine in the waiting room.

_____

_____

_____

_____

My second favorite household chore is ironing. My first being hitting my head on the top bunk bed until I faint.

Erma Bombeck

Housework

When I was a young, newly married woman, a book entitled *I Hate Housework!* was on the bestseller list. My now-faded copy with its cracked paperback spine is still on my bookshelf, and it is a treasure I will pass on to one of my grandchildren as a wedding gift.

My current theory about housework: the smaller the house, the less there is to clean. After my children left home, I moved into my current home, which meets my needs perfectly. I have to plug in the vacuum cleaner only once to vacuum my whole house.

I once heard that a messy bedroom is the sign of a messy life. When I reflect on different phases of my life, I have to agree that the statement is true. A trick I use to clean my bedroom is to put everything that is scattered around the room on my bed. Then I have to clean off the bed before I can go to sleep.

Being a responsible parent, I tried to get my children involved in housework. We tried different methods: posting signup lists on the refrigerator, rotating cleaning jobs, drawing for specific chores, letting the kids decide who would do what cleaning, and offering rewards. If you are waiting to hear which method worked the best, I'm sorry to disappoint you. Different methods worked at different times. It is interesting for me now to watch how my daughter handles this situation with her children. I must say, it is much more enjoyable to be the observing grandmother than it was to be the delegating mother!

During a stress-management class, I asked participants to name some things that they do to relax. One woman said she likes to iron. The group moaned! Another person said she wears a huge, baggy tee shirt with nothing under it and cleans. We all roared with laughter as we pictured her happily cleaning her house.

The lesson here is that there are people who find housework fun and relaxing. The next step for people like me is to get their phone numbers so I can invite them over to clean my house—to lessen my stress and theirs.

play·time

Make sure to choose pets that match the color of your tile and carpeting. No black pets for beige carpeting!

Schedule a party at your house. That will be the needed incentive to clean.

Keep lights low and use a lot of candles when entertaining so the guests won't notice the dust.

Wear a funky shower cap when you are painting or cleaning the ceiling fans.

Play loud, lively music that lifts your spirits while you clean.

Trade houses with a friend; she cleans yours, and you clean hers. It is easier to clean up someone else's mess, and you aren't there to see the house get dirty again.

Donate extra clothes and household items to your favorite charity.

De-clutter your house by inviting friends over to choose which of your unneeded items they want to take home.

Use environment-friendly cleaning supplies and count the hours you spend cleaning as volunteer time for the earth.

Have a garage sale where everything is a quarter. Things will move faster, and you will be helping people get what they need.

De-clutter your house by walking around a room with a basket and seeing how much clutter you can throw into it in five minutes. You can store the basket in a closet until you are ready to do deeper cleaning.

_____

_____

_____

_____

*Journal writing is a voyage
to the interior.*

Christina Baldwin

Journaling and Diaries

A few years ago, I spoke to a friend's fourth-grade class about being a self-published author. One of the children asked me how long I had been writing. I told her I started writing when I was ten years old. That year, I received my first "five-year diary" for Christmas. I don't remember specifically asking for it, but I do remember faithfully writing in it nightly for five years.

When I finished it, I started my second diary, which was forest green. I kept it hidden under lock and key, trying to hide it from my brothers, who threatened to read my secrets and tell them to the whole world. I kept special notations about what friends were saying about and doing to each other; boy friends that I had crushes on; records of athletic events that I participated in; radio and television shows that I was particularly fond of; gifts that I received for birthdays and holidays; and, of course, every disagreement that I had with my family. After all, I was recording history! I continued these diaries until I got married. I was then afraid that my mother-in-law was going to read these very private recorded thoughts and feelings—even if I did keep them under lock and key.

When I had children, I focused on writing in their baby books so they would have them for keepsakes. I recorded all of their "firsts," such as teeth, words, accidents, friends, birthday parties, and school activities. Each daughter has a very complete record of her first seven years. They tell me that they treasure their special books.

I got back to my journal writing when my children were teenagers. It was an outlet for many of my frustrations, dreams, and feelings. I must admit that I didn't write every day, but I knew that I had a way to vent privately when I needed to.

I regret that I did not journal during and after my cancer treatment. I can't think of a specific reason for skipping that period, but I do wish now that I had a record related to that time of my life.

Oprah encourages people to write "gratitude journals" as a way of reflecting daily on at least five positive things that happened during the day. I highly recommend this form of journaling as a way to live more positively.

However you do it, do it! You will stay in touch with yourself and feel better just because you take the time for yourself. And, after completing years of writing, you will have your autobiography almost ready to publish.

Journaling can be fun. Here are a few playful ideas. I am sure you can come up with more.

play·time

When your family goes on vacation, keep a trip journal of funny things that happen, places that you like and don't like, and anecdotes.

Write with different kinds of writing instruments and colors of ink, marker, crayons, etc.

Use a fancy book with special paper.

Draw funny doodles throughout your journal as you are thinking about what to write.

Don't criticize or evaluate what you are writing. Just write!

Put your pen to paper and write for ten minutes about whatever is in your head.

Help young children journal by writing their thoughts and feelings for them.

Buy diaries for adolescents so they will be encouraged to write.

Use a three-ring binder for a journal and decorate the cover.

Carry a small journal with you, so you can write while waiting.

Journal on your computer and hide it under a code name.

On vacations, do a group journal with different people writing each day.

Keep a play journal. Each night, write down five fun things you did that day.

_____

_____

_____

_____

*If enough meetings are held,
the meetings become more
important than the problem.*
    Susan Ohanian

Meetings

Most of us have to attend meetings for one reason or another. So we may as well learn how to have fun and be playful while we are in meetings. I hope that this section helps you to lighten your spirit during the meetings looming in your future.

I teach classes on how to facilitate effective meetings. Having fun and being playful during a professional meeting takes practice. Some people are very serious about their meetings, and they sometimes resent others who can have fun and still get things accomplished. But I don't let their attitude stop me. There's no reason we should all be miserable. However, one thing I am serious about is beginning and ending meetings on time. Lateness or lengthiness gives people a good excuse to be negative, and it's hard to have fun with a bunch of grouchy co-workers.

Meetings can be an organization's biggest money waster. I know about organizations that even have meetings about meetings!

I try not to attend meetings where I am just taking up space. Before I attend a meeting, I always ask myself what I can learn and what can I offer. Life is too short for us to spend time in any useless meetings. Some people attend so many meetings each day, that they never have time to do follow-up work. They must be the food seekers!

Some people look forward to meetings because they get free food. Even if the meeting is boring, they know they will enjoy the eating part. So, you might want to bring goodies to share. When I worked at a large childcare agency, departments took turns hosting meetings. When my colleague Tom and I facilitated, we won an award for hosting the shortest meeting of the year. Great food and short meetings! What else could anyone want?

The following playful ideas will help you look forward to your next meeting. Enjoy!

play·time

Add up how much money everyone is earning while they are at the meeting, and fantasize about how you could spend that money playing.

Bring a set of markers and doodle.

Bend a paper clip into a tiny person, and then name it.

Bring "fidgets" for people to play with during the meeting. (See suggestions under "Stress Relievers.")

Bring chocolate to share.

Offer people bubblegum to chew. When the meeting ends, have a bubble-blowing contest.

Prepare your dinner menus for the week.

Eat M&Ms and time how long it takes one to melt in your mouth.

Count the ceiling tiles while you do chin stretches.

See how many words you can make out of the letters in "procrastination."

Offer the chairperson your marker to use on the flip chart—the marker with the disappearing ink.

If you are responsible for handouts, glue some of the pages together and see how long people struggle to get them apart before they say anything.

Stare intently at the ceiling or at a spot on the wall and see how long it takes for everyone to figure out what you are looking at.

Carry pictures of your grandchildren to pass around.

Make a list of everything accomplished at today's meeting—if the page is blank, resolve to stop having meetings about that topic.

_____

_____

_____

_____

The one universal form of art is music.

Faith Baldwin

Music

Music gets our feet tapping and our lips humming. It can change a bad day into a good one. Research shows that even babies in the womb thrive when they hear music. At our local hospital, every time a baby is born, a lullaby plays over the public address system to welcome the newcomer.

Early care and education programs use music in many ways. Subtle music and lullabies play in the infant room; more energetic children's music keeps pace with the toddlers' high spirits; musical instruments clang and bang as preschoolers make up music; school-aged kids sing, play, and draw to music.

With this early exposure to music, it is no wonder that many of us use it for pleasure and entertainment. From attending a preschool holiday musical event to going to a symphony hall, we lift our spirits with music.

Music also connects us to others. During our annual vacation in Mexico, my friends and I always know it is a good omen when we hear Bob Marley's music telling us "every little thing is going to be all right." We nod our heads, sing, and dance when musicians fill the cobblestone streets with his music. Street musicians play in the open restaurants in Mexico. We stop our table conversations to appreciate the local talent. In cities around the world, street musicians perform. If you stop and enjoy the scene and the music, your day will be brighter.

On a recent trip, I purchased low-cost instruments so my friends and I can have our own mariachi band. You do not have to be a professional musician to enjoy playing the bongo drum, the maracas, or a set of bells. The band brings smiles to the amateur musicians and to everyone fortunate enough to be in listening range.

From childhood to old age, we can let music be a playful, joyful part of our lives. Try these activities to create fun with music.

play·time

Start your own kazoo band and participate in a community parade.

Make your own kazoo out of wax paper, an empty toilet paper roll, and a rubber band.

Play the oldies and see how many tunes you can remember.

Put a tree leaf between your two thumbs and blow, making a whistling sound.

Put sand or beans in a plastic Easter-egg container and shake to the rhythm of a song.

Make a clucking sound with your tongue.

Run your finger around rim of a crystal glass to make a humming sound.

Fill bottles up with different amounts of water and strike the bottles gently with a table knife or spoon to make different tones. Play a tune.

See how many songs you can sing that have the word "baby" or "love" in them.

Take two spoons, put them together between your knees, and play a tune.

Play "Name That Tune" with a friend by humming favorite children's songs.

Sing in the shower.

_____

_____

_____

_____

Breakfast is the one meal
where it is permissible to
read the paper.

Amy Vanderbilt

Newspapers

People can read the newspaper in a variety of ways. Some people read only certain sections. Others fold it carefully and read it column by column. Now it is even possible to read newspapers on a computer. I cannot imagine myself enjoying reading the screen with a cup of coffee. I prefer to read it the old fashioned way—by picking it up on my front porch, glancing at headlines, and reading what interests me.

Sunday morning newspaper time is a ritual in our family. We like to spread the paper all over the table. Certain sections go to select members of the family. The men rush for the sports, world, and business sections. The women enjoy the social, local, and entertainment sections. Ever since my children were little, the first sections they reach for each Sunday are the advertisements. Forget all of the news and current events; they want to know what's on sale so they can plan their shopping sprees. The funnies are up for grabs and are passed around so everyone can enjoy a good laugh.

I especially like a section called "Bulletin Board." This section features people's jokes, stories, and anecdotes. It is very casual and encourages people to contact the paper with their comments about daily living. The cute grandchildren stories are my favorites.

Another once-a-week section that draws my attention is health. It focuses on people who have changed their lifestyles in order to be healthier. Many of us use these human-interest stories for inspiration.

We have a very small local newspaper that gives all of the community news, with smaller sections for world activities. This newspaper is a great supplement to the larger, metropolitan paper. Without a doubt, newspapers contain something for everyone. Even my grandson enjoys asking the riddle, "What's black and white and red (read) all over?"

play·time

Sit on the floor and divide the paper by sections.

Make paper airplanes and have flying contests.

Make a homemade kite out of newspaper, sticks, and string.

Wrap gifts with the comic section.

Make up your own hidden-word contest.

Expand your vocabulary by completing the crossword puzzles.

Cut out your favorite cartoons and share them with friends.

Write a letter to the editor to express your thoughts and feelings on topics that matter to you.

Cut out articles of interest to a friend or family member.

Participate in contests that are sponsored by the newspaper.

Give your paper carrier a holiday bonus for a job well done.

_____

_____

_____

_____

Tropical nights are like
hammocks for lovers.
Anaïs Nin

Nighttime

As the day ends and evening begins, even the air feels different. During the winter season, night begins as early as 4:30 p.m.; in the summer, as late as 9:30 p.m. Whatever time it begins, night brings its own playfulness.

After dark, candles lit all over a room bring warmth and coziness. Scented candles add pleasant aromas. Candles are a huge industry all year, but sales soar as nights get longer!

You can create your own candles. My mother saved various shapes of tin cans and milk containers to use in her small candle-making shop in the unfinished basement. As children, we totally enjoyed the annual family candle-making event. And the candles made great holiday gifts!

At night, when things quiet down, you might go outside to look at the stars, sit in the dark and remember quiet times, or drink tea or other soothing beverages. You might ponder what you did that day that you are happy about, or what others in your life do that make you happy. You might quietly play in your thoughts, write down what made you laugh, or read a story to yourself.

A simple story read during the day, develops a different twist at night, in the dark. I remember hiding under my covers well past bedtime, reading books by flashlight. My imagination took me to many places in the world that were even more mysterious in the dim light.

Nighttime is a time for closure. Something is coming to an end. It is a time when we put aside boisterous daytime games to make room for more quiet and reserved play. Some people choose to spend their nights alone playing computer games, journaling, reading, listening to the radio, or watching television. Others spend nights with those closest to them.

Whatever you choose to do, you will probably notice that nights are a time for their own kind of fun!

play·time

Turn off all the lights in the house and play hide-and-seek, either in total darkness or with a flashlight.

Use a flashlight and your hand to make different shadow characters on the wall.

Fill a dark room with candles and your favorite music.

Write a letter in the candlelight.

Take a bath or shower with all the lights off.

Sit in a rocker by yourself or with a child and rock in the dark.

Gather with friends and tell ghost stories.

Do gentle stretching activities before bedtime.

Make your favorite dinner and allow yourself to go to bed without doing the dishes until morning.

Brush your pet and watch the static sparks fly.

Talk and laugh with a friend on the telephone.

Give your pet or other loved one a massage.

_____

_____

_____

_____

You don't stop laughing because you grow old; you grow old because you stop laughing.

Oldies but Goodies

On a recent summer vacation, my mother and I went shopping. My mother and I are very different sizes. She shops in the petite department; I do not. However, since my goal is to spend time with her, I followed along. On this particular shopping trip, I sat on the dressing room floor while she tried on her tiny clothes, asking me what I thought of each outfit. I got bored and started blowing bubbles that I just happened to have in my purse. "Act your age!" my mother said when she saw the delightful little bubbles floating across the crowded dressing room. "Age is only a collection of numbers," I responded. She reluctantly agreed and continued selecting her favorite clothes.

My friend's grandmother Gladys is eighty-eight years old and loves to play cards, play bingo, and go on outings with her friends. Twice a year, she and her friends hire a limousine to take them out to see the change of seasons. Their playful plan allows them to be together, laughing and having fun without any of them being responsible for driving. I believe that Gladys feels so healthy because she loves life. She can out-play many of her great-grandchildren.

My neighbor Merelyn's husband died this past year. Now, she has decided to take her five children and their families (twenty-one people) on a winter vacation. She enjoys playing with her children and grandchildren and wants them to have time together. She believes her husband would agree that the trip is a good idea. The family all understands that life is too short to put off opportunities to enjoy each other.

As we enter the twenty-first century, aging is becoming a profitable industry. Many companies offer playful experiences for seniors. They offer day trips and cruises, outings to cultural events, and lessons in everything from bridge to flirting. Gone are the days when people over sixty sat at home feeling sorry for themselves. Seniors laugh as they do water aerobics together or learn to tap dance. Older friends laugh together in coffee shops and restaurants. They join book clubs and volunteer. They walk together around a lake or sit on the swings on a playground.

They know it doesn't matter whether they play on an expensive cruise or at the local park. The important thing is that they enjoy life. Playing and having fun are ingredients for a healthy and happy transition to the last phase of our lives.

We can choose happiness and create fun ourselves at any age. Let's do it!

play·time

Agree with a friend your age to have weekly conversations that are just silly, proving that you never outgrow your need to have fun.

Have a monthly get-together with friends to celebrate birthdays. Focus on fun, not age.

Plan a "fun day," where spontaneity is the theme. Do whatever tickles your fancy, not what others might think is proper for your age.

Go to the park to enjoy nature and people. You can watch while you're sitting on a bench or walking on a path.

Go through your grandmother's jewelry box and wear your favorite piece.

Treat a younger person to an ice cream cone and have licking contests.

Have a conversation with a friend without talking about health-related matters.

Create a "wall of fun" that features pictures of you and your friends having fun recently and in the past.

No matter what your age, participate in the fun activities at the local community or senior center (skip the boring sessions).

Volunteer to be in a fashion show that benefits one of your favorite charities.

Strike up a conversation with a child (asking the parents' permission first).

_____

_____

_____

_____

The way I look at it, if the kids are still alive when my husband comes home from work, then I've done my job.

Roseanne

Parenting

When I think of the parenting that I did years ago, I use selective memory. Parenting is similar to childbirth. When one phase is over, we forget about the pain and remember the good parts.

I interviewed parents of young children about the joys of parenting. Many of them said, "Well, it depends on the hour and the day!" But then they smiled as they remembered funny stories.

Don't get me wrong. I firmly believe that being a parent is the hardest job in the world. As long as you are still breathing, you are still a parent. Our roles change, but nothing grabs a parent's immediate attention like a crying infant or the needy sound of your adult child's voice on the phone.

Those calls rarely come during the day. Usually the phone rings just after you settle in to watch David Letterman or just after you were finally able to fall asleep at 2 a.m. Our children may become adults, but they often need us in the middle of the night. Just as they did when they were infants.

Each phase of your child's development brings its own joys. When parents of preschoolers ask me, in worried voices, what it will be like when their children are teenagers, I tell them to enjoy their children now, and not to live in dread of what is to come.

There is the never-ending debate about which gender is easier to raise. Coming from a family with three brothers and then parenting two daughters, I say it's a tossup. Whether you have girls or boys, enjoy your children every day. Before you know it, you will be wondering where the time went.

Having a sense of humor while parenting is a necessity. I relied on the wit and wisdom of Erma Bombeck. She wrote commentaries about parenting for newspapers and magazines, and she turned mundane and frustrating events into comedy. She reminded me to put everything into perspective. Find someone who helps you laugh when parenting seems very serious.

I chose to be a parent, and I have never regretted it. Have fun with your children. Remember, they may decide where you live when you are old.

play·time

Read to your child before it is born. The child will begin to recognize your voice even before it leaves the womb.

Bring out your child's baby book from time to time.

Have a pajama day when there are no scheduled events and everyone can stay in pajamas all day long.

Develop a support network of friends who have children around the same ages as yours.

If children have a success or need some comfort, let them skip a day of school, and spend a special day together with them.

Set aside specific times (hours or days) that are reserved for quality family time.

Turn off the phone during family meals.

Go to a movie in your pajamas.

Paint your tennis shoes. Add glitter for a final touch.

Stop your work and sit down to play with your child.

Always have a loaded camera nearby to get those fun and spontaneous pictures.

Let the children plan the dinner menu. You cook whatever the child chooses (within playful reason).

During the celebrations of your child's graduation or wedding, show videos of childhood memories.

Get down on your child's level and pretend you are a cat or a dog. Don't forget to meow or purr or bark.

Set up a lemonade and cookie stand with your children.

Have your family participate in local community events such as parades, bike-a-thons, puppet shows, or community theater.

_____

_____

_____

_____

No animal should ever jump up on the dining-room furniture, unless absolutely certain that he can hold his own in the conversation.

Fran Lebowitz

Pets

I am a one hundred percent dog lover. I realize, however, that there are many playful pet possibilities. My friend keeps a rat and a hamster in her preschool classroom so her students can learn the responsibilities and joys of pet care at an early age. When I visit cat-loving friends, their pets peer around corners, come over and check me out, and then sit on my lap and purr. I can see why people like these independent but affectionate creatures.

Research tells us that petting an animal can improve our health. Interacting with a pet can lower blood pressure, lessen stress, and create a healthy emotional bond. Adult care centers often encourage visitors to bring the patients' pets for visits. Some nursing homes and children's hospitals have cats, dogs, birds, or bunnies. When my friend's daughter was hospitalized for pregnancy bed rest, her dog came for a short visit.

We don't need research to explain the benefits of relaxing, talking softly, and playing with pets. Between her many daily naps, my eleven-year-old cocker spaniel constantly gets her soft, squeaky, purple ball for me to throw. Playing with her always lifts my spirits. I cannot imagine my life without a pet.

Pets offer us a special loving, forgiving, and playful relationship. Use the following tips to add even more fun to your life with a pet.

play·time

Throw a pet birthday party and invite other similar pets. My cocker spaniel and I have hosted many very successful dog birthday parties, complete with hats, favors, and special treats.

Play hide-and-seek with a pet.

Make a collage with pictures of your pets.

Sit still and gently stroke your pet.

Lie on the floor and let your pet walk all over your body.

Have a race with your pet.

Tie a feather on a stick and invite your cat or dog to catch it.

Wad up small pieces of newspaper and toss them for your cat or dog to fetch.

Take your dog for a ride with you to places that give out pet treats (banks, fast-food drive-through windows).

Curl up and take a nap like a cat.

Like a cat, stretch out your body in a sunny place.

Get catnip-scented toys to use when you and the cat are both bored.

Watch videos for cats with your cats.

Put a bird feeder on a window where your cat likes to sit. Watch the birds together.

Get down on the floor and eat from a dish like your pet.

_____

_____

_____

_____

One hour with a child is like a ten-mile run.

Joan Benoit Samuelson

Playing with Children

Children are a wonderful source of energy, enthusiasm, and play-fulness. You don't have to be a parent or a grandparent to join children in their magical world.

My friend Pat doesn't have children, but young people are attracted to her like a magnet. Professionally, she has always worked with children. When she goes to a childcare center to observe one child, all of the children flock to her. They want to sit on her lap, hold her hand, tell her a special story, and most of all, be appreciated for who they are.

It is a great honor when children want to play with you. They size up a person's character pretty quickly. The best gift we can give in return is to be ourselves—especially our playful, childlike selves. Children are very trusting souls, and we need to respect their trust with our honesty.

If we want to learn how to play with children, we can learn from professionals who work in childcare facilities (schools, centers, homes) around the world. Observing these trained adults who are absorbed in child's play is a wonderful lesson.

My friend Vicki has taught young children for over twenty-five years. One of the things children love about her is her childlike personality. She really knows what children like and need, and so she enters their world as a trusted and compassionate person.

You are never too old or too young to play. We may think we are not very good at playing, but playing with children can change our minds. Children help us to remember there is no age limit for having fun.

If playing with children does not come naturally to you, here are some activities to help get you started.

play·time

Read a picture book without reading the words. Instead, you and a child can describe what is happening in the illustrations.

Let a child be the leader in a game of follow-the-leader.

Ask a child to sit on your lap and tell you a story.

Show interest in children's activities by asking open-ended questions and really listening to their answers.

Laugh with each other over silly rhymes you both make up.

Build towers of objects, and then let everything fall down when gravity takes over.

Pick bouquets of dandelions and make crowns for each other. Make a belly-laugh line with children. Lie on the floor and rest your head on the next person's stomach. Begin belly laughing.

Bring along your bag of toys when you go to play with children. They will enjoy seeing you and playing with your toys.

If you have known a child since birth, tell stories about the child's first days.

Make your own play dough or silliness putty and bring them along for your play date. (See the appendix for recipes.)

_____

_____

_____

_____

The smell of rain is rich with life.
Estela Portillo Trambley

Rainy Days

As the songs go, "Rainy days and Mondays always get me down," and "Rain, rain, go away. Come again another day." We can think of rainy days as depressing, or we can think of them as play days.

When we were children, most of us did not mind rainy days. In fact, they offered us opportunities to be spontaneous. When my friend Vicki was at her grandmother's house on a rainy day, Granny brought out her collection of used candles. Under Granny's supervision, the children melted candles on their own specially shaped bottles. At high school graduation, Granny presented each grandchild with her own rain bottle. Imagine how much wax and what wonderful colors covered those bottles filled with memories of special times together.

Growing up in Kansas City, I loved the special scent of rain in the air. Slugs often covered the sidewalks, so I tried to miss every slug when I walked home from babysitting. My brothers loved finding slugs and long earthworms to use for fishing bait.

On rainy days, we could choose to play inside or move outside to enjoy the weather. Few things are as lovely as a sweet, soft summer rain. Everything seems to look and smell so much fresher after the rain. It is as if Mother Nature washed the world.

Great big, sloppy puddles created joy. Rain boots made us feel playful and powerful as we jumped and splashed in the water. Sometimes we took our boots off and squished our toes into the cool mud. What great memories!

Rain, rain come today! We all want to play and play!

play·time

Curl up under a favorite blanket and read until you get sleepy, and then take a nap.

Bake or cook special comfort food.

Look for a rainbow.

Shop.

Run through or jump over puddles on the sidewalk.

Rent a favorite movie.

Take a walk in the rain, with or without an umbrella.

Paint a picture indoors, and then take it out into the rain to see how the rain blends the colors.

Float Popsicle sticks in puddles.

Let the wind turn your umbrella inside out.

Put a plastic sheet on a hill to create a "slip and slide."

Collect night crawlers for fishing.

Turn off all the lights in the house and run around with flash-
lights, screaming in delight.

_____

_____

_____

_____

Her dull mushroom eyes
seemed to have grown smaller,
as though they had been
sautéed too long.

Helen Hudson

Reading Glasses

As we age, our eyesight often begins to change or fail. I remember seeing this happen to my mother. There she would be in the grocery store, with her glasses around her neck, trying to read labels. I truly believed I would never be like that, but I am. I've decided that wearing glasses around your neck or perched on your head, is a rite of passage. You are telling the world that you are aging with style, grace, and fun.

I have found a way to have fun with my reading glasses. I buy fun and funky ones called "Peepers," which I find in gift shops and drugstores. When I am really lucky, I find them with tinted glass. Then I can look cool while I am reading outside in the sun.

Peepers come in many colors and styles. How many pairs of reading glasses should you have? Many. You need them all over your house, in your car, at your office, in your beach bag, in your purse, and perched on top of your head.

The chains that hold glasses around your neck can also be wild, unlike my mother's white pearl chain. Just a note, glasses chains are especially helpful to those of us who can't find the glasses that are sitting on our heads.

Think of the fashion plate you will be with your fun reading glasses and eyeglass chains!

play·time

Buy reading glasses in patterns and colors that match different outfits.

Put Peepers on stuffed animals or statues around your house.

Look for design noses made for reading glasses storage. Many gift stores sell these fun home accessories.

Have a Peepers cleaning party. Clean all of your reading glasses at one time.

Invite friends over to compare all your reading glasses. Give prizes for the most colorful, dramatic, practical, etc.

Find a special place to hang your reading glasses in your office, near your computer.

Wear your reading glasses low on your nose, like bifocals.

Swap reading glasses with friends.

Look for retro eyeglass chains in consignment and antique shops.

Wear two sets of reading glasses on your head and see how long
it takes someone to notice.

Make your own eyeglass chains
out of beads or seeds.

Put Peepers on your pets for funny photos.

_____

_____

_____

_____

In general, my children refused to eat anything that hadn't danced on TV.

Erma Bombeck

Restaurants

Some people who work in restaurants might want all of us to eat, pay, and move on. However, many establishments cater to playfulness. Playfulness might come dressed as a riverboat jazz band at an adult brunch or a clown blowing up balloons at a family restaurant.

One of my fondest childhood memories with my grandmother Meme is of going to a small, hole-in-the-wall restaurant in Detroit. We sat on stools around a horseshoe-shaped counter. When our order was ready, a small, slow-moving train chugged out of the kitchen carrying our sandwiches. It stopped right in front of us. We removed our lunches, and then the train circled back into the kitchen. It was quite a magical eating experience. I can't remember the restaurant's name. Maybe someone reading this book can refresh my incomplete, but vivid memory.

There are many kinds of restaurants. Fast-food places have indoor/outdoor playgrounds and free toys for children; family-style restaurants cater to families and friends who want a relaxed environment; ethnic cafes and coffee shops attract adults. Neighborhood bar-and-grills are informal, adult gathering places. Fancy tearooms specialize in pleasing women customers. Fine-dining restaurants cater to adults celebrating special occasions.

Any restaurant can make a dining experience fun and play-ful. Decorated tables, special party rooms, music, flowers, enter-tainers, paper placemats and crayons, outdoor patios, twinkling lights, and candles can make dining lighthearted.

Servers can be playful, and they often set the mood for the meal. In some restaurants, servers wear silly buttons on their uni-forms. In others, they might travel on roller skates. Many servers tell light jokes, compliment the diners, or talk about the special event people are celebrating. Some servers even sit in your booth while they take your order. Your playful attitude, in return, can spark more fun.

Let's look at some ways to have fun while dining out.

play·time

Go to a restaurant dressed in your favorite holiday costume.

Ask the servers to sing to the birthday person.

Bring a bag of stress-reducing toys to play with while waiting for your meal.

Order several dishes to share.

Share your dessert with your friends.

Play the spoons.

When the hostess says it will be a fifteen-minute wait, guess how long it really will be. Buy dessert for the person who guesses the closest.

Oooh and ahhh over the dessert menu. Order a favorite piece to split with a friend.

Watch sporting events.

Order something you've never tried.

If the restaurant offers chopsticks or suggests eating the food with your hands, pass up the fork and try it.

Look at people sitting at a nearby table and guess how they make a living.

_____

_____

_____

_____

Between threading a needle
and raving insanity is the
smallest eye in creation.
                        Caitlin Thomas

Sewing

Anyone who knows me will wonder how I can write about having fun with sewing. My main claim to sewing fame was a crudely crafted cross-stitch hanky I made when I attended a parochial grade school. I never did learn how to use the sewing machine.

I remember that my mother did attempt to introduce me to our Singer sewing machine when I was young, but I rejected the idea as I flew out the door to play kick-the-can with my neighborhood friends. My brothers, however, did learn how to sew on the machine. Fortunately for my mom, when my brothers' jeans tore, they were able to make their own repairs.

After I had children, I still had no idea how to operate a sewing machine, so I came up with a solution to my sewing problem. I stapled. I knew that I was on to something when surgeons began stapling instead of sewing in the operating room. When my children needed the hems shortened on their pants, I stapled. Then I covered the silver wire with ink that matched the color of the clothing. Eventually, I found out about iron-on tape. What a gift to sewing-challenged people like me!

One year, I did go through a sewing phase—I tried cross-stitching to make inexpensive gifts. I made many unattractive seat covers that never saw a chair, untidy pictures of birds and flowers that never got framed, and a special set of flags that I started for the Fourth of July but didn't finish until Labor Day.

I know that sewing is fun and relaxing for many people. My daughter loves it! It will be interesting to see whether my grandchildren follow in their mother's footsteps, or whether they carry their grandmother's impaired sewing genes. When sewing lessons begin, they might hop on their bikes and ride off to play. Or they might learn and then try to teach Nana a thing or two. If you are handy with a needle and thread, you might like to try some of the fun sewing activities that my daughter enjoys.

play·time

Meet monthly with a group of friends who like to sew, and learn from each other. At the same time, you can try out different cooking recipes.

Collect patterns and projects from Internet sites.

Sew gifts for friends and family (quilts, clothes, stuffed animals, and such).

Try out different home-decorating projects (for the bathroom, kitchen, bedroom, and living room).

Whenever you go somewhere and you anticipate a wait, take along your latest sewing project in a plastic bag.

Needlepoint greeting cards, pictures, or bookmarks to give to friends.

Collect funky sewing accessories to add fun to your routine (scissors, pin cushions, bobbin holders, etc.).

Collect, categorize, organize, and store fabric for fun projects.

Buy a basic sewing machine for a young person and teach him or her how to sew fun things (drawstring bags, funky pillowcases, etc.).

Plan a sewing project that you can start and finish in one sitting.

Let children pick out their own patterns for Halloween costumes, and then sew the costumes for them.

Create sets of matching towels, washcloths, and hand puppets for babies and children.

Sew a special outfit (baptism, bar mitzvah, communion) that can be worn and passed on to others in the family.

Make a wall hanging or quilt that represents your family tree and pass it on to other family members.

I am partial to the grocery store because it is one of the few places on earth where I can afford to buy pretty much any item I want.

Sarah Dunn

Shopping

Some people love shopping so much that it is always fun. Others put shopping at the bottom of their list of fun things to do. For all of us, there are times when we choose to shop and times when we must shop. Our attitude can make shopping a pleasure or a chore.

Given the choice, would you rather shop or clean the litter box? Does shopping relax you, or does it make you feel anxious and tense? This topic is for people like me who would rather drop than shop. How can we find ways to get the job done and even have some fun?

My youngest daughter, Carrie, loves to shop. She currently lives in a small community where there aren't many opportunities for playful shopping. As soon as she comes home to the big city for a visit, she shops! Carrie shops by herself, with her young nieces and nephew, or with friends. She is in her element in the shopping hustle and bustle.

When I shop, I want to make the experience as brief and painless as possible. I would rather spend quality time doing anything other than shopping. I usually avoid shopping malls, especially during holiday seasons. Shopping in the frantic holiday environment is extremely stressful. One way to reduce holiday stress is to stay out of the stores.

My oldest daughter, Kris, likes to order her family's food and necessities on the Internet. A day later, a yellow truck pulls up to her house and delivers the groceries. A relaxed Kris and happy children unpack the groceries together. Many people order toys, clothes, books, flowers, computers, and even furniture on the Internet so they don't have to deal with crowds and shopping.

We are living in a time when we have a choice about shopping. We can shop from home through catalogs, from the Internet, or by phone. Or, we can shift into our playful attitude and shop in stores. Here are some tips to help make shopping in stores fun.

play·time

Shop with a friend and try on bathing suits during the middle of winter. Laugh with each other!

Allow ample time to complete your shopping.

Plan to go out to eat after your shopping trip is done.

Go shopping with your pet at a pet store outlet.

Go shopping for bargains on the day after a holiday.

Go window-shopping.

Shop for people who are not able to do it themselves.

Try on larger clothes than you normally wear, so you feel thinner.

Shop at stores where everything is one dollar.

Shop at consignment stores. Someone else's trash could be your treasure.

Spend time at an exclusive store where the sales people choose clothes for you to try on.

Try on expensive jewelry and fantasize about where you would wear it.

_____

_____

_____

_____

To sing is an expression of your
being, a being which is becoming.
Maria Callas

Singing

One of the wonderful things about singing around children is
that they do not care whether you can carry a tune. My friend
Vicki, a nursery school teacher, wouldn't be able to carry a tune
to save her soul, but children love to sing with her. What she
lacks in melody, she makes up for in enthusiasm and positive
energy. Vicki loves to sing in the shower, in the bathtub, and in
the car. She even sings while she cleans her house.

Vicki once played a funny singing trick on her teenage son.
When Adam was thirteen, he often wouldn't get off the phone,
even after being asked several times. When he was talking to a girl,
the hours seemed to fly by. One day, after making several reasonable requests, Vicki resorted to singing. She picked up the exten-
sion phone and sang, "Oh, what a beautiful morning!" You can
imagine Adam's humiliation. He hung up the phone immediately.

When people sing, it is a sign of happiness and contentment.
One of my students in a directors' class sang in a gospel choir.

She said that when she was singing, nothing else in the world mattered. The choir helped her escape reality in a healthy way.

After retiring and moving across the country, my friend David joined a barbershop quartet and a church choir. Singing fills his days and evenings with joy and friendships. Whether we join formal singing groups or simply sing alone in the shower, singing improves our moods. Even when we sing at funerals, we can feel more peace and joy. Singing is free and accessible to you at any time. Don't be shy. Start singing today!

play·time

Make up your own songs.

Sing with children.

Sing with your dog and see whether you can copy each other.

Listen to "oldies" music and sing along.

Sing old camp or church songs and hymns.

Practice singing in the shower, in the car, or on a bike ride.

Go to a karaoke cafe and sing with friends.

Pick a category (trains, animals, etc.) and see how many silly songs you can sing about each topic.

Take singing lessons just for fun.

Join a community choir or musical.

Spend a whole day singing. Whenever anyone talks to you, sing back your response.

Answer the telephone while singing.

Sing with a group of friends and record yourselves.

_____

_____

_____

_____

It's no laughing matter, but it
doesn't matter if you laugh.
Jennie Gundmundsen

Smiling and Laughter

A book about play requires a chapter on laughter. Play and laughter seem to go together like smiling and laugh lines. You don't get one without the other. Did you know that it takes more facial muscles to frown than to smile? Did you also know that preschoolers smile about four hundred times a day, while adults average between seven to fifteen times a day? What happens to us?

When I was in high school, I was determined to get people to smile more, so I created a National Smile Day. I made and distributed smiley face stickers, and I asked everyone to wear the stickers to remind people to smile. People who smile are much more approachable than those who have a serious or grumpy face. Like most people, I prefer to be around people who are generally happy and have a cheerful disposition.

When I am doing seminars on laughter, I will ask people to look at the people sitting next to them and stick out their tongues. This usually gets them laughing and makes it difficult for them to finish the exercise. Then I ask them to curl their tongues. Not everyone can curl their tongue. The ability to curl your tongue is hereditary; laughter is not. Everyone can smile and laugh.

Smiling and laughing promote a feeling of well-being. Can you laugh at yourself? If you can't, it will be difficult for you to appreciate other people's humor. Many of us take life too seriously.

Smiling and laughing help balance out the intensity of life. When I work with people who deal with crisis every day in their personal and professional lives, I understand the importance of creating balance with laughter. There are so many benefits from laughter. Laughter reduces pain, reduces stress, is good exercise, attracts other people, makes the world a better place, and improves our quality of life. Laughing is free and accessible any time we need it. Just as it is impossible to feel stressed and relaxed at the same time, so is it impossible to feel happy and grumpy at the same time. Laughter is like attitude. We can choose it, and no one can take it away from us.

play·time

Rent a classic humor movie and laugh out loud at the slapstick comedy.

Read jokes and pass them on to friends through e-mails or letters.

Cut out funny cartoons from newspapers or magazines and put them on your refrigerator.

Keep a laughter journal of funny things that happen in your life.

Develop and maintain friendships with people who encourage smiling and laughter.

Mirror an infant or toddler's face as they go through their silly antics.

Buy and distribute funny stickers for everyone to enjoy.

Attend a conference and look for humor workshops.

Sing a silly song to a child.

Write down funny things children do, and give the notes to their parents.

_____

_____

_____

_____

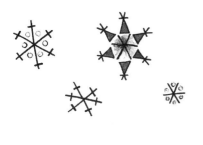

I am younger each year at the first snow. When I see it, suddenly, in the air, all little and white and moving; then I am in love again and very young and I believe everything.

Anne Sexton

Snowy Days

Children and playful adults glow with happiness when it snows. The earlier in the season snow falls, the better. A new snowfall adds brightness to gloomy winter days. A soft white blanket covering the dry ground, the snow beckons us to come out and play. I know many readers are not fortunate enough to have snow in the winter. But then you have other perks. I've lived in three Midwestern states, so snow I know.

Snowy days create fond childhood memories. Young children love to feel, roll in, and toss the snow. Grade-school children love to make forts, snow people, and snowballs. Teenagers and

college students love snow days so they can catch up on lost sleep or go skiing.

In the early 1990s, a huge snowstorm shut down the entire Twin Cities metropolitan area for days. Even adults loved this blizzard, because it gave us an excuse to stay home. We retreated from our hectic schedules and stayed safe and warm. Or we went outside and played like children.

We can enjoy snowy days at any age. I have seen many rigid and uptight adults become childlike when there is a great snowfall to clear. Shoveling the driveway can be fun, and it is great exercise if you are in good shape. Building snow mountains, shovelful by shovelful, is an empowering experience. Using a snow blower to help neighbors is fun for owners of this awesome winter toy.

Children of all ages can play in the snow with sleds, saucers, toboggans, snowmobiles, snowshoes, cross-country and downhill skis, and four-wheelers. Here are some more ways to feel playful on snowy days.

play·time

Lie on your back in the snow. Move your arms up and down, and in and out to make snow angels.

Start a snowball fight.

Make snow ice cream. Avoid yellow snow!

Stick out your tongue and catch snowflakes.

Build a snow fort.

Shovel a path and have others follow you.

Hop like a rabbit to leave unusual footprints.

Squirt food coloring on snow. Make creative designs.

Spray colored water on snow forts, igloos, and sculptures.

Make a snow family and dress them with items from your
wardrobe.

Go for a walk in the snow and enjoy nature.

Take black-and-white photos to show how beautiful your snowy
world is. Send copies of the pictures to those less fortunate
people who do not experience snow where they live.

_____

_____

_____

_____

The test of being a good host is how well the departing guest likes himself.

Marcelene Cox

Social Events

For centuries, women have gathered in each other's homes for quilting parties; bridge games; book clubs; teas and coffees; sewing circles; and for parties to sell kitchenware, food, baskets, or candles. Women often plan parties to celebrate special events such as weddings, christenings, and graduations. I've even attended a party to celebrate a person's life after they had died. The goals of these events is to have fun and to be with other people in a comfortable setting.

Although many social events focus around women, men also attend couples' events such as pre-wedding showers, birthday clubs, family events, and gourmet cooking clubs. They enjoy male bonding without women at bachelor parties, sporting events, support groups, and card nights.

At many social events, everyone sits in a circle. Not on little carpet squares like we did as children, but in circles just the same. In some circles, one person may present ideas while others listen. At others, there may be several conversations going on. But somehow, a circle creates friendship. As social beings, we enjoy the camaraderie of others. Often people in groups express a variety of emotions. These emotions can be contagious. Soon many in the circle join in with another's laughter or tears.

Of course, good food is usually part of a social gathering. Sharing food is a universal way of welcoming and being with people. We can measure the success of a social event by how the guests feel as they leave. Are they truly glad they came, or do they leave feeling they were not part of the group? Having playful moments during a gathering, no matter how serious it is, will help insure that most people will relax and feel as if they belong.

Let's look at some of the ways that you can enhance social events to raise the level of enjoyment and fun.

play·time

Decide on a theme and decorate your home in interesting and fun ways.

Have nametags that say how the person knows the guest of honor or host(ess) of the party.

Wear silly items that accent the theme of the party.

Plan special activities for the beginning of the party so people will get to know each other.

Have a theme party where everyone dresses to match the theme: animals, states, colors, foods, etc.

Offer door prizes to the person who gets to the party first, the person who comes the farthest, the person who has known the host(ess) the longest, or the person whose birthday is closest to that of the guest of honor.

Decorate a chair especially for the guest of honor.

Fill goodie bags with treats for the guests.

Put names of famous people on the guests' backs. Each guest then asks the others questions about the famous person until they guess who they are for the night.

Pass popcorn around the circle.

Ask people to bring the recipe for the potluck dish they bring and enough copies to give to each guest.

Take Polaroid pictures of your friends in funny poses.

Play musical chairs once. When the music stops, everyone sits down and you have an instant circle.

What sunshine is to flowers,
smiles are to humanity.
Joseph Addison

Strangers

How many close friends do you have now who were once strangers? Everyone I know, outside of my family, at one time was a stranger. That fact makes the risk of meeting someone new appealing. Although I give talks to thousands of people, I often fear walking over to a stranger and striking up a conversation.

Back in the 1950s, I attended dance school. A group of thirteen-year-old girls and boys came together dressed in their finest clothes to learn the social graces of interacting and dancing. The girls stood against one wall, and the boys, the other. When the instructor insisted, the boys sauntered across the room and asked the girls to dance. We girls waited patiently. If we weren't selected, we would try to act as though it was not a big deal. But it was! Fortunately, I survived this time in my life. But, as silly as it may seem, dance school reinforced my fear of meeting strangers. I sometimes feel like that thirteen-year-old girl again, afraid of being rejected.

Fortunately, I usually remember that I am an adult now. And throughout my life, I have met some very delightful people who were strangers but who are now very dear friends. It is worth the risk to speak to people you do not know. Put on a smile, and be fun and playful. If someone chooses to join your fun, you know that you can connect, at least at one level.

You and I are probably strangers. I invite you to connect with me by e-mail, the telephone, or in person. Let's have some fun together and demystify the fear of meeting new people.

play·time

Before you attend a social event, decide how many strangers you are going to meet.

At your child's athletic function, begin a conversation with another parent.

When you meet people who only want to talk about work, ask what they like to do for fun.

Take your dog to a leash-free park and talk to other dog owners.

Attend a conference and make a point of connecting with at least three people you didn't know before.

At a crowded restaurant, sit at a table with another single person.

Online chat with strangers about a common interest.

Deliver cookies to a neighbor, a shut in, or an elderly person.

Coordinate a block party to meet your neighbors.

Offer a piece of candy to strangers who you meet while waiting (on the bus, for a meeting, at the park).

Compliment strangers on their clothing.

When you move into a new neighborhood, invite neighbors over for a barbeque or a cup of coffee.

_____

_____

_____

_____

Stress is an ignorant state. It believes that everything is an emergency.

Natalie Goldberg

Stress Relievers

Over the years, I have learned that there are many ways to relieve stress. I remember, when I was very young, watching my grandmother twiddling her thumbs. I'm not sure she was aware of what she was doing, but as she twiddled her thumbs, I saw her face soften. This was the first time I can remember seeing someone use their body to reduce stress. Then I noticed my father crossing his legs and methodically swinging his foot. My friend twisted her hair while she read a book. Do you have any relaxing habits similar to these?

As a professional adult in my early twenties, I needed to incorporate a little fun into my office life to help reduce the stress. I began collecting children's toys that adults could enjoy. When I spun a little plastic top, played with a puppet, or built a short block tower on my desk, I relaxed. After my short recess, my work didn't seem as stressful as it did before I played.

My toy collection grew. When I began doing workshops on stress management, I had a large bag of toys, including Slinky toys, bubbles, blocks, and tops for my presentations. I let the participants play as they listened to me, so they could have fun while they learned.

You do not have to spend a lot of money on your stress toy collection—you can even use household items. Remember that the toys should be tactile and relaxing. To make great stress-reducing toys, you can combine some of the following items in zippered plastic bags or in sealed pouches: food coloring, salt, sugar, shaving cream, hair gel, gelatin, pudding, cooked instant mashed potatoes, cooking oil, flour, balloons, smooth stones, rubber bands, or glitter. Children who are ages three and over, love to help you make these toys. Just look through the activities listed below, and then make some fun!

play·time

Carry bubbles at all times and blow them for instant stress relief.

Carry a key chain that has little toys attached to it.

If salt or sugar spills, draw or doodle in it.

Collect a bag of colorful stones to decorate your home or office.

Use a few stones as worry stones that you rub in the palm of
your hand.

Carry a paper and colored pencils or pens to use for mindless
doodling.

Make a "fidget bag," which contains many materials you can
play with: rubber bands, small fuzzy balls, miniature Slinky
toys, plastic twisting coils, paper clips, and small containers
of play dough.

Check the Web for sites that sell various stress toys. (See the
appendix.)

Fold a paper airplane and sail it across the room.

Drink out of a bendable funny straw.

Keep a hand puppet in your desk drawer. Take it out for playful
conversation times.

_____

_____

_____

_____

The leap up of the sun is as
glad as a child's laugh; it is as
a renewal of the world's youth.
Margaret Deland

Sunny Days

When we think about sunny days, we might imagine warm summer days, complete with lemonade and bathing suits. Indeed, those are good days. But, I believe that sunny days are awesome at any time of the year. In fact, when the weather is less than perfect, I appreciate a sunny day even more. I live in a part of the country where it is more often cold than warm. When it is fifteen below zero, the weather is more tolerable when the sun is out. The world is more beautiful when those sunny rays push through the clouds.

When I was younger, I collected funny pins with sayings such as "Be Kind To Me, I Have Teenagers" and "Desperately Seeking Sun." When I wore these pins, people nodded, smiled, and said, "I can relate." Now, I hang a bright royal-blue flag with a brilliant yellow sun on my porch to show the world I love the sun. Even on cloudy days, my flag waves in the wind, cheering up the entire neighborhood.

The sun positively affects our attitudes. It lifts our moods. We are happier and more open to playfulness when the sun is shining. Seasonal affective disorder (SAD) is a debilitating syndrome that affects millions of people. The treatment is to go out into the sun or to use a light box.

As a hospice volunteer, I give primary caregivers a prism after a loved one dies. Our program encourages caregivers to hang the prism in a window so the sun can reflect from the cut-glass edges

to make rainbows all over the room. The rainbows signify the many ways the deceased person touched the lives of the people left behind. This tradition brings joy and happy memories whenever the sun shines.

Can you imagine a guided imagery session beginning, "Picture yourself lying on a beach under a cloudy sky"? Why not? Probably because we realize that the sun helps us to relax and feel good.

I think of the sun as warm, inviting, healthy, energetic, and happy—playful adjectives. I see children skipping down the sidewalk, teenagers riding bicycles down the road, adults out walking their dogs—all with sunny dispositions.

Promise yourself that you will enjoy, really enjoy, the next sunny day that comes along.

play·time

Buy sunscreen that comes in playful colors.

Watch your shadow move as clouds pass over the sun.

Sit and watch sunlit clouds. Name various shapes in the beautiful formations.

When the sun comes out after a summer rain, look for a rainbow.

Sit outside under a shady tree and watch how nature changes as the sun moves throughout the day.

Guess what time the sun will rise or set.

Remember the childhood saying "Red sky at night, sailors delight. Red sky in the morning, sailors take warning," and find out whether it's true.

Try to follow a butterfly's erratic flight.

Try to guess the time of day by the location of the sun.

Hang prisms in your window and watch the rainbows.

Hang a simple piece of stained glass in a window and enjoy the
colors when the sun shines through it.

_____

_____

_____

_____

*No leader can be too far
ahead of his followers.*

Eleanor Roosevelt

Training Large Groups

Working with groups of one hundred people or more can be as fun as it is challenging. Many companies, schools, and other organizations provide training for large groups. Often, the employees are required to attend the training. Some attendees come to simply listen and won't join in activities; some take this opportunity to catch a quick nap; and others learn by actively participating. It is important that, as trainers, we recognize people's differing interest levels and learning styles. To be effective trainers, we must know how to work with adult learners. There are books in the library that will offer you tips on this topic.

Have you ever noticed while watching the evening news, how quickly topics change? The media understand that we have short attention spans. Research tells us that adults can focus for only six minutes at a time. What a challenge for trainers and educators who are attempting to relay information!

The first step a trainer must make is to relate with the audience. What techniques help them to connect to us? Humor is a universal connector. We don't have to be stand-up comics, but we can use storytelling, funny commentary, and jokes. The audience response will let us know what is working. When the audience is laughing, we know they are listening.

I recently attended a required refresher driver's education class. I was not looking forward to spending two eight-hour days listening to information I already knew. To my pleasant surprise, the instructor was funny, casual, and informative, and he presented the mundane material in a way that we senior adults enjoyed. By the end of the classes, I did learn things I hadn't known. The trainer's skill helped me change my negative attitude and open up my learning channels.

Although some messages cannot be conveyed in a playful way, most are enhanced with some humorous additions. Incorporate some of the following tips to make large-group training more valuable to those sometimes reluctant adults sitting in front of you.

play·time

Use appealing graphics on your overheads, slides, or PowerPoint presentations.

Share favorite cartoons that apply to your topics.

Invite participants to share their comments at appropriate times.

Offer prizes to participants in different categories (newest employee, most experienced, etc.).

Get people's names or business cards as they enter, and use them for drawing door prizes.

Pay attention to participants' nonverbal messages. When you notice that they are losing focus, call for a "stretch time."

Have everyone take a few deep breaths when their attention wanders.

Build in time for people to share ideas with the people sitting next to them.

Use self-disclosure exercises appropriate for the topic and audience.

Use storytelling to engage the audience. Everyone likes a good story.

_____

_____

_____

_____

You take people as far as they will go, not as far as you would like them to go.

Jeannette Rankin

Training Small Groups

I try to teach the way I would like to be taught. You can read about adult learning styles in many publications. In this book, I offer you some ways to have fun while you train others. If you have fun, the participants probably will, too. Remember, a relaxed learner is an eager learner.

Some adults can pay attention longer than children, and some cannot. Recently, I taught a class for childcare directors. When one of the directors introduced herself, she said she was used to moving around the room with children. She wasn't sure how long she could sit still. I needed this information, because it validated the importance of the small-group activities I had planned for the class. Another director brought colored markers, and she let everyone know that doodling helped her to concentrate. Again, it was good for us to know what her needs were.

No matter how long your training session is, pay attention to the participants' needs, and accommodate as many needs as you can.

Everyone feels the need to be involved. One way to involve participants is to invite them to plan the training session. You can have an open agenda and let participants list what they want to discuss. Or, you can ask the participants to voice their expectations for the training. Then, you can adjust your plans to accommodate their needs.

Planning playful activities will help your training immensely. Relax and model what having fun while learning is all about. Here are some ways to incorporate play into your small-group training sessions.

play·time

Get local merchants to donate door prizes.

Bring special treats for participants to munch on during the session.

Provide "fidgets" for participants to play with. (See suggestions under "Stress Relievers.")

Use evaluation forms on which participants can draw faces that reflect how they felt about the class.

Have participants decorate their own nametags.

Start each training session with an active icebreaker that is relevant to the topic.

Give a prize to the first person who arrives at the training.

Ask participants to tell why they are at this training. All answers, even the fact that it is a bad TV night, count.

Let the participants leave fifteen minutes early. No one has ever complained about leaving early.

Use brightly colored markers on the flip chart.

Provide participants with well-designed and fun handouts.

_____

  _____

_____

  _____

*A vacation is having nothing
to do and all day to do it in.*
Robert Orben

Vacations

A really great vacation is one that generates stories that you retell for years. The vacation may seem horrible at the time, but the stories you remember make up for the misadventures.

Many years ago, I went on a two-week vacation with my friend Vicki and her two boys. Because Vicki's husband needed to stay home and work, I was elected to be the second adult. Everything that could go wrong did go wrong. It rained day after day. Kids and dogs tracked mud into the cabin. Because we couldn't go outside, we ate tons of junk food. Chip bags and candy wrappers everywhere!

Our aching stomachs only added to our misery. We were all grumpy. Even then, we laughed a lot, knowing that if we didn't laugh, we would cry. Vicki called the trip a test of our friendship. I think we both passed. And, oh, the stories we still tell.

Of course, there have been many delightful vacations. They also provide lasting memories. When my children were young, I decided our family needed a yearly vacation to ease the five-month winters. Each year, I took the kids out of school for a week, so they could do experiential learning while our family bonded in warmer climates. After twenty years, those vacations still bring up "remember when?" storytelling.

Vacations do not have to be expensive to be considered great. When our family was contemplating a major relocation from Missouri to somewhere north, we stayed with friends for a few days. Our friends took us to parks and rivers. It was a wonderful family time that we will never forget.

Perfect or not, vacations can be fun to remember. Can you remember some of your favorite vacation times? Here are some suggestions for creating fun and playful times with family, with friends, or even by yourself.

play·time

Pop some popcorn and watch the movie *Family Vacation*.

Bring vacation snacks that combine sugar, salt, and protein.

Start off on your vacation without a specific destination in mind.

Grab a backpack and go on a mini-vacation that is a getaway just for you.

Plan a vacation that celebrates a special event (anniversary, birth-day, etc.).

Go to the library and check out travel books to help you plan your vacation.

Plan a vacation that takes you back to places you visited as a child.

Visit relatives in different parts of the world.

Keep a travel journal that highlights the fun places you visit and the funny stories you will want to remember.

On the way home, ask all of the vacationers to name the trip's high points and funniest events.

_____

_____

_____

_____

Where there is laughter, there is always more health than sickness.

Phyllis Bottome

Visiting the Doctor

Many people become terrified at the thought of seeing a doctor. They may have had stressful previous visits. Or they don't know how to be themselves with the person who is in charge of their health and speaks in a language that is difficult to understand. I find that when you treat doctors the way you treat other professionals, there is nothing to fear. Sure, they are capable of producing more physical pain than attorneys or teachers, but it helps to remember that you both have the same concern: your health.

You are more apt to feel nervous when you see a new doctor. Fortunately, I have had the same primary physician for twenty-three years. He was only in his late twenties when I started seeing him. From the beginning, he has listened. Dr. Jeff encourages his patients to call him by his first name. When he comes through the door, his relaxed, caring, and empathetic nature walks in with him. Dr. Jeff talks and laughs with his patients, setting them at ease. It is clear that he is concerned and that he will do whatever it takes to address his patients' problems.

My friends and I all took our adolescents to Dr. Jeff for his famous talk on "sex, drugs, and rock and roll." Dr. Jeff and other medical professionals prove that humor has a place in a medical office. If you currently see a doctor you cannot relate to in a relaxed, professional way, why continue the relationship?

One caution for us good-natured, funny, easy-going patients to remember is there are times to be playful, but there are also times to be serious. While I was healing from cancer, I learned to balance my relationship with many medical professionals so they would take me seriously.

Patch Adams is a great movie in which Robin Williams plays a physician who uses humor to lessen patients' stress and fear. Patch Adams is a real person. He helps us realize we can be playful even if we are in pain. Following his lead, we can use humor as patients. Perhaps if we give medical professionals permission, they will be happy to lighten up while they help us to live longer.

play·time

Bring something fun to do in the waiting room. You might want to bring humorous books, handheld games, comedy CDs, snacks, bubbles, or stress-relieving toys.

Draw cartoon figures of other patients who are waiting. Draw cartoon bubbles that show what they are thinking.

Include markers in your supply kit for the examining room. Draw pictures on the white exam table paper.

Collect comics or cute stories related to medicine and share them with your physician.

Bring some recent magazines to replace the old ones at the clinic.

Bring an old pair of oven mitts to put on the stirrups for more gentle foot care.

Discuss health and humor with your physician.

When the nurse asks you to step on the scale, reply that you do not participate in self-defeating activities.

Wear a different hat or funny socks each time you go to the doctor.

_____

_____

_____

_____

There is more to life than increasing its speed.

Gandhi

Waiting in Line

Waiting in line can be boring, frustrating, and a waste of time. "Hurry up and wait" is often the story of our lives. If this is our attitude, maybe we can learn from people who wait in line for days to purchase a ticket to a concert or sporting event. These folks have a great time while they wait in line. Some bring sleeping bags, lawn chairs, portable televisions, food, and musical instruments. They playfully meet other people who are comrades in their adventure.

I heard about one couple who met waiting in a line. After they purchased their tickets, they went on their first date, and they eventually got married. They probably enjoyed the reception line at their wedding! This couple certainly proves that some things are worth the wait.

Sometimes you wait in line in your car. Even in this stressful situation, being playful can take the pain out of waiting. If your family is with you, you can enjoy the luxury of uninterrupted conversation. Instead of phones ringing, the TV blaring, and people running out the door, you have a quiet time to have fun together. Tell jokes or old family stories, blow bubbles, or really talk.

Very young children shouldn't have to wait in long lines. However, try as we may, sometimes there we are, in line with children. There are creative ways to make these situations easier. For example, while others are in the bathroom, the waiting children can engage in other activities. They can listen to stories, sing songs, or play word and counting games. It is important for children to learn how to take turns, but they can also learn that it can be fun.

We cannot avoid all lines. So, wherever we are, or whomever we are with when we end up in a line, we can be playful. Here are some tips to stimulate your creativity.

play·time

Carry a small notebook and pen, for instant doodling.

Make lists of playful things you will do when you are no longer in line.

Call a friend on your cellular phone.

Meditate and take yourself to a more relaxing place.

Count the number of people who are waiting behind you. Be grateful that you are ahead of them.

Bring out your bubbles and let others share in your fun.

Carry a book to read or your journal to write in.

Start a joke-telling contest with the people around you.

Make up stories about the people around you.

Eavesdrop on other people's conversations.

_____

_____

_____

_____

*My grandmother started walking five miles a day when she was sixty. She's ninety-seven now and we don't know where the he** she is.*

Ellen DeGeneres

Walking

Walking is free and instantly available. You can walk by yourself or with friends. And, if you are blessed with good health, you can walk nearly all of your life. Best of all, walking can be fun!

Sometimes I prefer walking alone, totally immersed in nature. I remember taking many walks alone in the woods, down dirt roads, or along sandy beaches to relax and clear my mind. I generated many of the ideas in this book during walks with nature.

When I want to take a long, healthy walk, it is easier to walk with a friend. At an agreed-upon time, very early in the morning, I call and wake up my friend Deb. When I walk this early in the morning, I can hide my bed-head under a baseball cap, and I can wear any old outfit! Early-morning walkers are not out to impress others with their stylish clothes. They want to get the walking done so they can move into the rest of their day feeling good. Walking with another person makes the time and distance pass more quickly. And the commitment to a friend is a great motivator when I want to roll over and hit the snooze button.

If the weather is inclement and you can't get outside, you can walk in place in your house while you watch TV, you can walk in a mall, or you can go to a local health club and use the treadmill. At health clubs, people often read their favorite magazines or chat breathlessly with friends.

Walking a dog is fun any time of the day. My friend Vicki and I love to take our cocker spaniels walking in the woods where leashes are not required. The dogs are happy running about, and Vicki and I have a chance to visit. Walking your dog is also a great way to meet people. Dog lovers are usually friendly and love to talk about their pets.

Whether you walk alone or with your friends and your pets, the main point is to have fun. Being able to walk is a physical gift to be appreciated and enjoyed.

play·time

Guess how many steps it will take to walk to a specific tree or building.

When you walk in the sand, vary your stride and observe your footprints.

Walk blindfolded, guided by a friend.

Walk in a maze.

Play follow-the-leader with a group of children.

Play follow-the-leader when no one is following.

Sing silly songs or whistle while you walk.

Walk your dog and see how many different breeds of dogs you meet.

Get down on your hands and knees, and try to walk like a dog.

Walk on a sidewalk and see how many cracks you can avoid.

Go on a nature walk and collect shells, leaves, sticks, and other interesting things.

Go on a trash walk and see how much you can improve the environment. Make a collage or a sculpture with some of the trash when you return.

Pack a picnic snack, and then walk somewhere by yourself and have a picnic.

_____

_____

Water Play

We can play with water in something as small as a glass or as large as an ocean. All water moves in mesmerizing ways. Sitting by a lake, creek, or ocean can enthrall us for hours. Even water spilled on the floor forms interesting shapes, if we take the time to notice.

I have been attracted to water since I was a baby. It is hard for me to feel depressed around water. A stream or river is as relaxing as an ocean is powerful. Floating on an air mattress, allowing the current to sway me back and forth, is relaxing and fun. My passion may be genetic, because my children and grandchildren love the water, too. Or it may be nurtured, because my siblings and I were all introduced to swimming at very early ages. Because I am a swimming instructor, my daughters were in the pool as soon as their umbilical cords fell off. In the summer, we always had a plastic swimming pool in our small back yard.

My friend Mary and I have taken women's groups to Mexico for weeks of fun and relaxation. Our favorite memories are of

groups of adult women splashing, playing, and doing water aerobics in the beautiful blue Caribbean. These groups of professional women set their titles aside and played like young children,
without any cares or concerns about others' judgments. Likewise,
when I see my brothers in a swimming pool playing with their
children, I realize that they are the same men their professional
colleagues see at work, but they look quite different having fun
in water.

I am fascinated by some of the stress-reducing toys I have
that use water. Sometimes, toys have colored water that turns a
small water wheel or drips in soothing ways through a maze.
When water and oil meet, the water looks lazy as it sloshes
through the container.

In preschool programs, children love the water table, which can be filled with soap bubbles, with toys to float or sink, or with dishes that need to be washed. Whether you are washing dishes in your kitchen or jumping the waves in the ocean, water can bring you joy and relaxation.

play·time

Fill a glass with water. Slowly stir the water as you add drops of food coloring and observe the changes.

Play the "sink or float" game. Ask a child to guess which objects will sink or float when placed in water.

Add oil and food coloring to water and watch what happens.

Turn on the outside hose and have fun squirting each other.

Run through a sprinkler in your yard.

Float poker chips in the water and swim after them.

Dance in the water to songs such as "Hokey Pokey," "Humpty Dumpty," or "Ring around the Rosie."

Play active games in the water such as tag, Red Rover, and follow-the-leader.

See how long you can hold your breath under water.

Float on your back and name the cloud designs floating overhead.

Curl your body up into a ball and float like a turtle.

Swish sticks through water and listen to the sounds.

Fish.

Take a nap while you float in a rowboat.

Put on your favorite bathing suit and float down a river in an inner tube.

_____

_____

_____

_____

In my studio, I am as happy as a cow in her stall.

Louise Nevelson

Workplace

People work in many different kinds of places. You may work in your home, at a desk in a classroom, in a Dilbert-like cubical, in a storage closet at a gym, or in a huge office suite. No matter what your workplace is, you can be respectfully playful at work.

I once worked in a large agency that gave prizes for special offices. There was a prize for the neatest office, the most cluttered office, and the cheeriest office. They awarded me a prize for having an office the most like a college dorm room. I had motivational posters on the wall, stress toys on my desk, and my children's drawings nestled everywhere. Memorabilia from my travels filled my bookshelves.

Now, I have an office in my home. The walls are fire-engine red, symbolizing creativity, energy, and passion. Fish mobiles hang from the ceiling. Prisms in the windows create rainbow reflections in the room. I display my grandchildren's artwork on the walls. And, of course, intriguing stress toys sit next to my computer.

When I visit other professionals at their workplaces, I look for clues to their personalities. Some offices contain no personal items, while others are decorated with family pictures, trip mementos, and small treasures from children. Look around your place of work. Is it a place that you enjoy going to? Does it send a message about who you are as a person? Are there things that you would like to change?

Let your creativity flow and make your workplace playful.

play·time

Create a wall mural with notes of appreciation people send to you.

Have children make colorful handprints on the wall.

Hang posters of nature scenes.

Use a Mickey Mouse telephone.

Fill your office with toys and activities that reduce stress.

Organize different dress days: beach day, sub-zero day, casual day, backwards day.

Celebrate birthdays with gusto.

Have potluck days. Everyone brings food to share at lunch.

Bring in a humorist to speak at a staff meeting.

Allow people to have a holiday on their birthdays.

Create a gratitude tree. Co-workers write positive comments about each other on green construction paper leaves and attach them to the branches.

Create a staff appreciation bulletin board.

Use a whiteboard for brainstorming ideas that create positive motivation.

_____

　_____

_____

　_____

APPENDIX

Suggestions to enhance play time!

BATHTUB PLAY • 14

Bath Salts Recipe #1

1 cup sea salt
1/2 teaspoon glycerin
1/2 cup Epsom salts

Mix ingredients well. Sprinkle into bath water anytime you
   need to be rejuvenated!

Bath Salts Recipe #2

2 cups Epsom salts
1/2 teaspoon food coloring (if desired)
1/2 to 1 drop essential oils
1/2 cup dried rose petals, crumbled to near powder

Mix all ingredients. Makes lovely bath salts. Package the mixture in a favorite bottle. Or put it in a canning jar and
   decorate the lid for a special person, season, or holiday.

Bath Salts Recipe #3

4 cups Epsom salts
2 cups sea salt
1/2 to 1 drop essential oils
2 tablespoons glycerin (if desired)
1/2 teaspoon food coloring (if desired)

Mix the two salts together to use as a base. Scent two cups of the mixture as desired. Glycerin will soften skin, but place a warning tag that reads "Not for use in whirlpool baths." Store in a zippered bag for two weeks, shaking daily. After the two-week period is up, pour the salts into pretty jars.

Bathtub Finger Paints

1/3 cup clear liquid dish soap
1 tablespoon cornstarch
food coloring (as desired)

Mix liquid soap and cornstarch together in a small bowl until blended. Pour the mixture in equal amounts into an ice cube tray. Add a couple of drops of food coloring into each compartment and mix. Do not let little ones get this finger paint into their eyes.

BUBBLES • 25

Bubble Solution (in a gallon jug)
    2 cups Joy dishwashing detergent
    6 cups water
    3/4 cup Karo light syrup

Combine, shake, and let settle four hours before using. (For
    best results, use only Joy and Karo.)

MEETINGS • 78

Baloney Bingo
Here's a fun game that was passed on to me by a friend:

1. Before (or during) your next meeting, seminar, or conference call, prepare your "Baloney Bingo" card by drawing a
square. Five inches by five inches is a good size. Divide it into
twenty-five one-inch squares, five across and five down.

2. Write one of the following words or phrases in each
square: synergy, strategic fit, core competencies, best practices,
bottom line, revisit, take that off-line, 24/7, out of the loop,
benchmark, value-added, proactive, win-win, think outside the
box, fast track, result-driven, empower (or empowerment),
knowledge base, at the end of the day, touch base, mindset,
client focused, ballpark, game plan, leverage.

3. Check off the appropriate square when you hear one of those words or phrases.

4. When you get five squares horizontally, vertically, or diagonally, stand up and shout, "Baloney!"

PLAYING WITH CHILDREN • 103

Play Dough

    2 cups flour
    1 cup salt
    1 teaspoon cream of tartar
    2 tablespoons vegetable oil
    1 teaspoon food coloring
    2 cups water

Mix ingredients in a saucepan. A grown-up should always help with the stove. Cook over medium heat, stirring constantly, until the mixture leaves the sides of the pan. Remove the mixture from the pan and let it cool. When the mixture is cool to the touch, knead it for a few minutes. Store in an airtight container.

Silliness Putty

    2 parts Elmer's White Glue (1/2 cup)

    1 part liquid starch (1/4 cup)

Mix well and let dry enough so that it is workable.

STRESS RELIEVERS • 137

Here are some websites that feature toys that you can use for "fidgets" or stress toys. If you would like to find more toys, try out your favorite search engine and enter "stress toys."

    www.officeplayground.com

    www.oriental.com

    www.smilemakers.com

    www.promowebsite.com

    www.tangletoys.com

    www.getmotivated.com

ABOUT THE AUTHOR

Sue Baldwin is the owner of INSIGHTS Training & Consulting in Stillwater, Minnesota. She has a degree in counseling and her work experience in administration, childcare, teaching, and training.

Sue's family consists of two adult daughters, Kris and Carrie; son-in-law, Tim; grandchildren, Nick, Anna, and Ellie; and cocker spaniel, K.C. Throughout the years, she has learned compassion and humor in her relationships with family, friends, colleagues, and pets.

Sue is avidly involved with hospice families and volunteers, and she has a strong grasp of the skills necessary to interact with people at all stages of living and dying. Sue also teaches swimming for infants and preschoolers throughout the year. She has been a cancer survivor since 1997 and believes that having fun, being playful, and creating balance helps contribute to a healthy and full life.

ABOUT INSIGHTS TRAINING & CONSULTING

Sue Baldwin started INSIGHTS Training & Consulting in 1994. Since 1982, she has trained nationally and internationally on topics related to personal and professional development. The participants in Sue's training sessions enjoy her sense of humor and informal teaching style. Her methods make it easy for participants to learn how to make changes for themselves and enhance their careers. Her topics include "How Can I Idle My Motor When I Feel Like Stripping My Gears?" "Lighten Up and Live Longer," "Building a Better Team," "Little Spats and Huge Disputes," and "Communication Is More Than Just Talking."

INSIGHTS Training & Consulting offers the publications listed below. An order form appears on the following page.
Lifesavers: Tips for Success and Sanity for Early Childhood Managers

ISBN # 0-9654439-0-6 $14.00
Lighten Up and Live Longer – A Collection of Jokes, Anecdotes, and Stories Guaranteed to Tickle Your Soul

ISBN # 0-9654439-1-4 $12.00
The Playful Adult: 500 Ways to Lighten Your Spirit and Tickle Your Soul

ISBN # 0-9654439-2-2 $15.00

For more information about INSIGHTS Training & Consulting, please visit our website at www.suebaldwin.com.

ORDER SUE BALDWIN'S BOOKS

Quantity	Title	Amount
	The Playful Adult • $15.00	
	Lighten Up and Live Longer • $12.00	
	Lifesavers: Tips for Success and Sanity • $14.00	
	Subtotal	
	MN Residents Add 6.5% Tax	
	Shipping & Handling	
	TOTAL	

Your Address:

Name:_____

Address:_____

City:_____ State:_____ Zip:_____

Phone:_____ E-mail:_____

Shipping Address (if different from yours):

Name:_____

Address:_____

City:_____ State:_____ Zip:_____

Phone:_____ E-mail:_____

Shipping and Handling: If your subtotal is up to $24, add $2.95; if $25–$49, add $3.95; if $50–$75, add $5.95; if $76–$99, add $7.95.

Quantity discounts are available.

Print this form and send it with your check or money order to:
Sue Baldwin, INSIGHTS Training & Consulting, 2559 Hawthorne Lane, Stillwater, MN 55082-5266.